Praise for *Learning* in the *Workplace*

'No one asks or answers the tricky question "How can I implement LT successfully in my organization?" Now finally someone has. We have some practical, concrete and exceptionally clear answers here that should not be ignored. This book could save you time, money and a lot of embarrassment. Go read it.' **Nigel Paine, International Speaker and Author,** *The Learning Challenge*

'Anyone engaged in workplace learning will benefit from reading this book. Drawing on plenty of real-world examples, it spells out clearly what L&D professionals need to do when looking to extend their focus beyond the classroom and into integrating learning technologies.' **Charles Jennings, Co-founder, 70:20:10 Institute**

'This book illustrates a key fact of learning and performance tools – that making them work has very little to do with the technology and almost everything to do with the people involved. These tools are just that. Having a hammer doesn't make one a carpenter. This book speaks to the key factors we need to adopt to bridge this gap and get the most out of these valuable resources. Highly recommended!' **Bob Mosher, Learning Advocate, MASIE Center**

'There is enough rhetoric around leveraging SMAC (Social, Mobile, Analytics and Cloud) within enterprise learning. This can mean putting together a comprehensive learning architecture that could include enterprise social platforms, contemporary LMS, mobile learning apps, simulations, virtual reality tools, and so on. Donald H Taylor focuses on the leadership, maturity and mindset required to launch and embed these disruptive ideas within enterprise learning. He also highlights the skills required to champion new ways of working that must be built on a robust understanding of organizations' internal reality and context.' **Sunder Ramachandran, General Manager – Training, GlaxoSmithKline Pharmaceuticals India**

'The future of learning at work is blended and increasingly informal. No one is better placed than Donald H Taylor to understand both the opportunities and the practical approaches needed to overcome the numerous obstacles in our path.' **Clive Shepherd, Founding Director, The More Than Blended Learning Company**

'Since 2003, Towards Maturity's benchmark research has shown how learning innovation can, and does, deliver business impact. It has also uncovered that many L&D professionals struggle to understand the tactics necessary for success. Donald H Taylor combines his pragmatic experience with research and case studies to explore good practices in learning technology implementations and has created a must-read for everyone involved in the process.' **Laura Overton, CEO and Founder, Towards Maturity**

'So much of modern workplace learning relies on technologies and yet nobody has written a definitive guide to their implementation – until now. It's readable, insightful and useful and I recommend it.' **Jane Hart, Founder, Centre for Learning and Performance Technologies**

Learning Technologies in the Workplace

How to successfully implement learning technologies in organizations

Donald H Taylor

KoganPage

First published in Great Britain and the United States in 2017 by Kogan Page Limited

2nd Floor, 45 Gee Street
London
EC1V 3RS
United Kingdom

c/o Martin P Hill Consulting
122 W 27th St 10th Floor
New York, NY 10001
USA

4737/23 Ansari Road
Daryaganj
New Delhi 110002
India

www.koganpage.com

© Donald H Taylor, 2017

The right of Donald H Taylor to be identified as the author of this work has been asserted by him in accordance with the Copyright, Designs and Patents Act 1988.

ISBN   978 0 7494 7640 3
E-ISBN   978 0 7494 7647 2

British Library Cataloguing-in-Publication Data

A CIP record for this book is available from the British Library.

Library of Congress Cataloging-in-Publication Data

Names: Taylor, Donald H. (Donald Helmdon), 1963- author.
Title: Learning technologies in the workplace : how to successfully implement
   learning technologies in organizations / Donald H. Taylor.
Description: London ; New York : Kogan Page, [2017] | Includes
   bibliographical references and index.
Identifiers: LCCN 2017005912 (print) | LCCN 2017015141 (ebook) | ISBN
   9780749476472 (ebook) | ISBN 9780749476403 (alk. paper)
Subjects: LCSH: Employees–Training of. | Educational technology. |
   Organizational learning.
Classification: LCC HF5549.5.T7 (ebook) | LCC HF5549.5.T7 T296 2017 (print) |
   DDC 658.3/1240284–dc23

Typeset by Integra Software Services, Pondicherry
Print production managed by Jellyfish
Printed and bound by CPI Group (UK) Ltd, Croydon, CR0 4YY

CONTENTS

PART ONE
The learning technology landscape

A learning utopia?

01

Most people know nothing about learning. THOMAS MORE, UTOPIA, ENGLAND, 1516

I get that we have to do this, but why do they gotta make doing it so hard? 'SALLY', STARBUCKS, NEW YORK, UNITED STATES, 2013

In January 2013, David Kelly, a technology-focused learning and development specialist in New York visited his local Starbucks to get some work done. It was a crisp winter's day, and he was enjoying getting into the rhythm of work with his favourite large tea at his side when his concentration was broken by the person sharing his table making a call on her mobile phone (Kelly, 2013). She was staring with annoyance at her computer, open in front of her.

'No,' she sighed in exasperation into her phone, 'I'm able to sign into the laptop. I just can't get signed into the training.'

Once her colleague had talked her through accessing the training system, she sat at her keyboard, staring at her screen, mostly bored, occasionally frustrated, as she repeatedly clicked the 'Next' button, which moved her e-learning course on.

After about 90 minutes, she called her colleague again. She had to leave the café and wanted to know whether it was possible to leave the course halfway through, because, as she put it, 'I don't wanna have to go through all this again'.

David felt he had to know more. As soon as she had finished her conversation and shut her laptop, he introduced himself, explained who he was, and asked what was going on. Her initial reaction was to put some distance between herself and someone who came from the profession who had made her life hell for the previous hour and a half. Assuaged by a caramel macchiato and the promise of anonymity, 'Sally' explained that she was taking a mandatory course. It was almost the same course as the previous year.

'Maybe you can explain to me why I have to take the same course year after year?' she asked in understandable frustration.

Every year her organization updated the course to reflect changes that employees need to know, and updated the test, too, to include those changes. Sally appreciated the need to be aware of the changes, but not the way the information was conveyed. 'I know they want us to take the whole course,' she said, 'but wouldn't it be easier to also tell us what's changed so we can be on the lookout for it?'

In was not only the content of the course that had riled her – repetitive, with the important changes buried amid the familiar and trivial; it was not only the nature of the course itself, which consisted of reading screens of information and clicking the 'Next' button to progress; it was also the process of getting to the course, through a system that needed a separate login, different to her regular login for the company systems. On top of all this was the frustration that this 'training course' had nothing to do with learning. 'We don't learn anything from these,' she said, 'and everybody knows that. They just want to know that it's done.'

A committed employee just trying to do her job, Sally summed up her frustration in a single question: 'I get that we have to do this, but why do they gotta make doing it so hard?'

Sally's experience is not unique. Too many employees experience the combination of a tedious course with non-intuitive software. Too often the content they are exposed to seems neither relevant to their job, nor to have much to do with learning. And too often it seems to have little to do with the business, either.

It doesn't have to be this way. At the 2014 Learning Technologies Conference in London, a case study from major UK healthcare provider HC-One included a short video of care worker Kate Cairns, who had been through the company's *touch* programme. This programme, which we'll hear more about in Chapter 9, was designed to support an ambitious cultural change programme and relied heavily on e-learning. The reaction of those in the programme, in contrast to Sally's, was overwhelmingly positive. 'E-learning has been great for me,' Kate said in a matter of fact way, 'but also great news for the residents. I don't have to leave my shift to do my training. It gives me more time to spend with the residents, which is why I'm here.'

Other staff agree. Well over 95 per cent of a survey of 4,244 employees said that *touch* had given them new knowledge and understanding, and over 90 per cent felt the programme had given them more control over their learning and development. In addition, over 90 per cent of managers said that the programme had increased competence and not just compliance ratings (Innes-Farquar, 2014).

We will see other, similar examples in this book where learning technologies have been implemented well, in ways useful for employees, help learning and add to the value of the organization.

Most adults have always understood the value of learning (Thomas More, whose quote opens this chapter, did when he wrote *Utopia* 500 years ago). The vast majority of employees certainly understand it, and know its importance for their work. Learning technology offers a promise of easy access to engaging, accessible learning content. The frustration for employees, therefore, is that our understanding of learning's importance and the promise of learning technology too often does not translate into anything effective. On the positive side, the use of learning technologies does seem to be improving, but inconsistently and slowly. This book is an attempt to identify and spread good practice more widely, and so protect people from Sally's frustrating experience. Employees deserve better. They deserve a learning utopia, not the dystopia it too often turns out to be.

In writing this book, I talked to many people who use learning technologies well. I looked back over 16 years of case studies from the Learning Technologies Conference. I explored case studies from other sources, too. In the course of all this, it became clear that successful learning technology implementations are not a matter of chance. By the same token, failed implementations usually happen for reasons that are predictable and preventable. To understand why these errors are so common, and so often repeated, we need to travel back in time to 1999, to the height of the dot-com boom, when learning technologies were in their infancy, and one influential man in particular was predicting a great future for them.

References

Innes-Farquar, A (2014) *Supporting performance with technology and showing its impact*, Learning Technologies Conference, 29 January

Kelly, D (22 January 2013) [accessed 22 November 2016] *What do people *really* think about that course you've designed?* [Online] http://davidkelly.me/2013/01/what-do-people-really-think-about-that-course-youve-designed/

How did we get here?

02

Education over the Internet is going to be so big it is going to make e-mail look like a rounding error. JOHN CHAMBERS, CEO OF CISCO SYSTEMS, SPEAKING AT COMDEX 1999

The COMDEX information technology exhibition of November 1999 was one of the largest IT events ever staged in the world. Over 200,000 attendees flocked to Las Vegas for five days of information technology heaven. Those were heady times. The information technology sector was riding high on a dot-com boom, which had driven the NASDAQ stock market to five years of spectacular growth. In a fervid atmosphere, vendors pitched their products and services and, in the huge main auditorium, industry luminaries led by Microsoft chief Bill Gates delivered their vision of the future (McCann, 1999).

When Cisco's John Chambers stepped up to the podium on the third day, he introduced to the general public a term that had only been used previously by specialists: 'e-learning'. The term was so new that in its reporting CNN put quotation marks around it, comparing its potential with the explosive impact of the newly arrived e-commerce (D'Amico, 1999a).

In his keynote address, John Chambers was prophetic about the future of learning technologies when he said that education over the internet would be huge. He was, however, wide of the mark on the detail, including the speed at which it would happen. Similarly, COMDEX did a good job trailing the future in places, with a watch-phone from Samsung and discussions on the importance of open software. The event, though, also featured set pieces from then-dominant companies such as Novell and Corel, which have long since been sidelined, and a complaint from Hewlett-Packard CEO Carly Fiorina that for too many people the internet was still 'too foreign, distant, cold and threatening'. Fiorina correctly saw the need for a more familiar, friendly internet; she probably did not foresee how quickly it would arrive or the impact it would have (Schwartz, 1999; Sykes, 1999).

For what neither Carly Fiorina nor John Chambers nor almost anyone at COMDEX could have foreseen was how the internet – or more precisely the world wide web that sits on top of the internet – would blow apart the existing, centuries-old model of how we understand and handle information, and the wide implications of that change.

Chambers was the head of one of the world's largest and most successful software infrastructure companies, a savvy operator and visionary, he was one of the reasons behind its success. But in his speech he overestimated the likely pace of change in the use of technology in learning, even though he correctly identified one major hurdle to its adoption. Pointing to the education system, he said that the technology to support learning was already there. The key roadblock to adoption was that many teachers didn't like to surrender to students the power to decide what to learn. In contrast, he suggested, over the coming two years, training would become a continuing process as companies educated their employees via the internet (D'Amico, 1999b).

In that speech, Chambers identified a key issue – that using technology for learning threatened an existing, entrenched system of what he called 'command and control'. He also exhibited a technologist's typical over-optimism about what can be achieved in a short timescale of two years. But he missed one important thing – something that probably nobody could have predicted. Once the internet stopped being 'foreign, distant, cold and threatening', the genie was out of the bottle. People were going to use the internet for learning anyway, whatever their company, their teachers or anyone else told them (D'Amico, 1999c).

In this book we will return time and again to three themes illustrated in that significant keynote. The first: that mental models of learning based on traditional schooling dominate and limit our thinking. The second: that people, not technology, will determine the pace and quality of learning technology implementations. The third point is the most fundamental: that the way we deal with information has been changed forever by technology. From being a rare commodity, it has become super abundant. And the time taken to build personal connections – our route to much of our knowledge – has shrunk from years to minutes thanks to social media. The impact on us personally, and on the places we work, is profound. It enables us to learn in exciting new ways, but it also challenges deeply the mental models we use, particularly those that equate learning with schooling.

The promise of learning technologies

The early promise

By the time of Chambers' speech in 1999, electronic learning technologies were nothing new. Mass-produced, school- and consumer-focused computers had been in use for over two decades, led by the first consumer computers: the Commodore PET, launched in the North American market in the late 1970s and in the UK its equivalent, the BBC Micro, released to market in 1981.

These desktop computers were, by today's standards, extremely simple, using cassette tape to store programs and having far less processing power than a modern mobile phone or even smart watch. Basic though they were, the machines introduced an entire generation to information technology (IT), and in particular to its use for learning. One Commodore PET advert carried a picture of a teacher and the slogan 'PET. The Microcomputer that's top of its class', while government subsidies and a thirst for technology meant that by 1986, 80 per cent of the schools in the UK had a BBC microcomputer of some sort. By 1999, the audience that John Chambers addressed were primed for the idea of e-learning. They had been brought up on it (Old Computers, 2016; Wikipedia, 2016a; Vasko, 1986).

There was an alternative to this technology-led approach that began with a computer and then looked for ways it could be applied in the classroom. This alternative was exemplified in the UK by a company set up in 1972 by a small group of television professionals including John Cleese, of the British comedy group Monty Python. Video Arts Limited produced short films that made their points dramatically and humorously and were created with high production values. (Typical titles included: *Meetings, bloody meetings* and *The unorganized manager*.) The company is still in operation, having successfully changed distribution media from video cassettes to CDs to the internet. This longevity is in marked contrast to many other providers of technology and e-learning, and is in part at least due to its focus not on the technology used, but on creating pithy content that makes its point with humour, and is filmed to the same standards as broadcast-quality television. As John Cleese is quoted saying on the company's home page: 'People learn nothing when they're asleep and very little when they're bored.'

This emphasis on the nature of how people learn is unusual in an industry where companies have traditionally focused not on content itself, nor on learning, but on technology and on the distribution of content.

Early learning technologists concerned themselves only with their particular technology, imagining that training was largely about taking information, parcelling it up into digestible chunks and distributing it to people who then, somehow, learned it. Successive technologies, it was claimed, would handle one, or both, of the parcelling up and the distribution.

This pattern has been repeated for a series of technologies from the phonograph, through radio and television to virtual worlds and MOOCs (Massive Open Online Courses). Each was trumpeted as *the* technology that would variously transform education, make teachers/trainers superfluous and so on. Each has failed in this transformation (although for more on MOOCs see Part Three); usually they end up becoming an ancillary tool to a regular programme of instruction.

Sometimes individual learning technologies grew extremely sophisticated in what they could deliver, as with the videodisc, which in 1980s offered a rich, interactive medium for instruction and learning. These were all, nonetheless, individual technologies. It was the advent of the world wide web in 1989 that laid the foundations for today's learning technologies, and for the cover-all word that would be coined to describe them.

Founded in the mid 1980s, CBT Systems was ahead of its time in offering computer-based training (hence the CBT). When they became widely available, the company moved to CD ROMs for distribution, and achieved a dominant position as a technology learning provider. Towards the end of the 1990s it had over a thousand courses on its catalogue, 95 per cent focused on IT. It also, crucially, had helped to create Unisys University, which delivered personalized training over the web to employees and partners, tracked activity and provided discussion groups and more. This project was a powerful demonstration of the future of technology-supported learning in contrast to the uncertain fortunes of CD ROM-based distribution. In 1998, the company missed its revenue projections, and president and CEO Greg Priest did not hesitate. Realizing that the web was the coming delivery mechanism, he staked CBT Systems' future on this new business model and a new identity. In October 1999, one month before Chambers' speech, the company announced its new name and its new strapline: SmartForce, The eLearning Company (Cross, 2004).

This was not the first time the word e-learning had been used (or elearning, or eLearning, as it was also variously styled in those days). It was, however, the first time it had been used as part of a branding exercise for a major corporation. In November 1999, as Mark Penton and I were finalizing the conference programme for the January 2000 Learning Technologies Conference in London, we briefly considered whether to run a session entitled 'What is elearning?' We decided quickly that there was no need. The term was in established use. However you spelled it, 'e-learning' was here to stay.

The 21st-century promise

Although in the 21st century information technology has developed massively, the understanding of the role of learning technologies has not. In general, it is still regarded simply as a way of being more efficient in delivering these two simple promises of storing and distributing information.

At the very beginning of the millennium, it was the distribution part of this that everyone was fixated on, as epitomized by that term 'e-learning'. Nobody could miss the obvious power of the internet. In comparison with the administrative and technical overhead of distributing courses on CD ROMs, the idea that it would be possible to reach people almost instantly, at their desks (nobody was thinking about mobile channels yet), seemed an instructional nirvana.

Then two things happened close enough to change how learning technologies were sold, used and – crucially – how they were viewed.

The first was that in March 2000, the US technology stock market, the NASDAQ, peaked at just over 5,000 points. This was the high point of a spurt of dizzying growth. Five years earlier it had been below 1,000 points. That rate of growth could not last forever, and it didn't (even though analysts were predicting the 'new economy' could hit 6,000 points by the year end). On 10 March, the dot-com bubble burst, sending the NASDAQ into a 27-month tailspin that saw the market lose over 70 per cent of its value (CNN Money, 2000; Wikipedia, 2016b).

All technology companies were hit. Giants such as Microsoft lost over half their stock value within the year. But at least they were solvent and profitable. Newer companies, which had attracted investment on the hopes of future profits, found their stock prices next to obliterated – losing 80 per cent to 90 per cent of their market value. Those that survived the initial shock needed a way to establish their value fast. So, too, did employees who had seen their stock options wiped out overnight.

In the learning technology sector, companies needed a clear sales proposition. They found it in cost savings, dressed up in the fancier guise of Return on Investment (ROI). (The dressing up was not always accurate; see Chapter 9 for more on measuring value and ROI.) The pitch was compelling: learning online would be as good as classroom training, but delivered far more cheaply without the need for classrooms and trainers, and no need for delegates to travel – saving both time and money.

This proposition – that learning with technology was cheaper than the classroom – had been in play for some of the 1990s, but as the technology markets slumped, so pressures on travel budgets grew and the cost saving offer grew more compelling.

The second major incident for learning technology was the by-product of a much larger event: the terrorist attacks on New York's World Trade Center twin towers on 11 September 2001.

Beyond the 9/11 attacks' immediate, terrible human toll was a lasting economic impact. Companies in the United States and Europe were already suffering after the dot-com crash. US growth was slow and Europe was in recession. Aiming to protect staff and further reduce expenditure, many companies slapped outright bans on all corporate travel. Immediately after the attacks, air travel in the United States dropped by 30 per cent and airlines didn't wait for the bad news. Just nine days after the attacks, British Airways cut 7,000 jobs, other airlines did the same (Logan, 2007; BBC News, 2001).

The US economy stuttered. COMDEX's attendance fell to just 124,000 as travel budgets were axed. Above all, corporations cut training – as they always do when times are hard – and did not invest in e-learning nor anything else. As the economy floundered, all investments were put on hold, with training systems close to the bottom of the list of priorities.

In these straightened circumstances, learning technology providers clung to the prospect most appealing for corporates looking to cut costs: e-learning could deliver training faster and cheaper. The result was a single, coherent message from learning technology providers, a message that was to last several years and echo even longer. E-learning, that new term, which John Chambers had told us would transform the future, that bright vision of tomorrow, became something altogether more practical and perhaps a little grubbier – a cheaper way to get your training done.

Many of the courses produced in this time – and since – were of poor quality. Designed to parcel up and distribute information, they removed instructors, replaced them with nothing, and required the learner to do little more than click to the next page of the course, where they would be presented with more information, and perhaps – if they were lucky – a test. 'Click next' training, as it became known, gave e-learning a reputation as boring, unpleasant, unengaging material that continues to this day. In the 2015 Learning Survey from the Learning and Performance Institute (LPI), of nearly 500 people surveyed, only 6 per cent rated 'Generic, self-paced elearning' as delivering high student satisfaction. The figure for 'Formal face-to-face courses' was the highest of all 11 media considered: 47 per cent.

The schoolroom assumption

The legacy of those long years when learning technologies were seen only as a cost-cutting measure is that e-learning was for a long time regarded as a cheap substitute for the classroom, the 'poor man's' training, rather than a medium that has something to offer in its own right.

This history has been a major influence on thinking about e-learning. There is, however, another, ever more important, influence on how we think about learning as a whole. It is particularly significant for anyone seeking to implement learning technologies: our experience of learning over the first 15 or so years of our lives.

Most people view learning through their experience of the schoolroom and the course. And because this experience is near universal across all ages, classes and geographies, it goes unchallenged and unrecognized. It simply manifests itself as an assumption – that all learning requires the teaching of new material. This may not necessarily be done in a classroom, but in the minds of most people – whether employees, managers or executives – it certainly should be done via a course, just like it was at school. I call this the schoolroom assumption.

Sometimes a course is, indeed, the right response to a learning need, whether it is delivered by a person or through electronic self-study. That is particularly true when the subject matter is new. It can also work where you know something, but need to expand and deepen that knowledge. So new recruits to an organization are frequently put through onboarding courses, and employees are frequently subjected to compliance courses.

However, these instances are only two of what Bob Mosher and Conrad Gottfredson call the five moments of learning need (Gottfredson and Mosher, 2011):

1 When people learn something for the first time (New).

2 When people expand what they have learned (More).

3 When they need to act upon what they have learned (Apply).

4 When problems arise (Solve).

5 When people need to learn a new way of doing something, which requires them to change skills and ingrained practices (Change).

Moments 3 to 5 – when we need to act or change what we are doing – make up most of the learning we do at work, and are seldom best tackled with a course. And yet, because of the schoolroom assumption, the first reaction of many managers and employees on seeing a performance problem is to apply a course, even though most of these moments of need are best dealt with using a range of alternatives – from coaching, to expert advice to performance aids, to crowd-source problem solving.

Yet it is the schoolroom assumption that exerts the most power pull on the imaginations of executives, managers, employees and even many in the Learning and Development department. This is unsurprising. Classroom instruction is all we know in the formative years of our lives. Our parents – no matter their backgrounds – had exactly the same experience in the first years of their lives. During our childhood, they silently reinforce the schoolroom assumption over every breakfast and dinner. When we first go to work, we find ourselves in a large group of people where everyone else has had exactly the same experience – from the person at the top to the lowliest employee, from the old stager to the young buck, and most likely the first thing we experience at work is an induction process, which begins with us sitting, as we have done for the previous 15 years or more, at desks, facing an expert at the front. And all of this has been going on certainly since mass education was made compulsory in the late 19th century, drawing on a tradition that stretched back to the foundation of the first modern university – the University of Bologna – in 1088. If you wanted to indoctrinate an entire population, this is how you would do it.

Is it any wonder that the power of the schoolroom assumption over our unconscious minds is so strong? And think what that assumption brings with it: the power structure of the classroom (quiet, obedience and deference to an expert), the habit of keeping your work to yourself, and the sense that learning is a chore to be undergone, that happens at a particular place and time.

This is not to say that the classroom or the course is always the wrong choice, only that it is not always the right choice and that despite this, it continues to be the unconsciously assumed default method for dealing with learning. As we will see in the next chapter, this is despite the fact that we learn at work in a myriad of different ways, and only occasionally in the classroom.

Key takeaways

1 Technologists often underestimate the time it will take for technology to fulfil its potential.

2 Learning has long been misinterpreted as little more than the packaging up and distribution of things to learn (or 'content').

3 In contrast, others recognize that to learn from content, it is essential to engage with it, not merely be presented with it. Emotions and humour help with this.

4 In the early 21st century, two major events shifted how e-learning was sold to the world: the dot-com crash and the 9/11 attacks on the Twin Towers in New York.

5 After these events (and to an extent before them) e-learning was positioned as the low-cost alternative to classroom training, rather than something new with merits of its own.

6 This approach was aided by a long-standing misconception – the schoolroom assumption – that learning equates to a course, usually taken in a physical space.

7 In reality, courses, classrooms and training are not always the best ways of learning, as suggested by Gottfredson and Mosher's five moments of learning need.

References

BBC News (2001) [accessed 22 November 2016] British Airways cuts 7,000 jobs, *BBC News*, 20 September, [Online] http://news.bbc.co.uk/1/hi/business/1553676.stm

CNN Money (2000) [accessed 22 November 2016] Nasdaq sets record (again), *CNN.com*, 10 March, [Online] http://money.cnn.com/2000/03/10/markets/markets_newyork/

Cross, J (2004) [accessed 22 November 2016] An Informal History of eLearning, *On the Horizon*, **12** (3), pp 103–110 [Online] http://www.internettime.com/Learning/articles/xAn%20Informal%20History%20of%20eLearning.pdf

D'Amico, M L (1999a) [accessed 22 November 2016] Cisco head sees e-learning as next wave, *CNN.com*, 17 November, [Online] http://edition.cnn.com/TECH/computing/9911/17/comdex.elearning.idg/index.html

D'Amico, M L (1999b) [accessed 22 November 2016] Networking CEO predicts e-learning wave, *Info World*, 6 December, [Online] https://books.google.co.uk/books?id=vU4EAAAAMBAJ&pg=PA67

D'Amico, M L (1999c) [accessed 22 November 2016] Cisco head sees e-learning as next wave, *CNN.com*, November, [Online] http://edition.cnn.com/TECH/computing/9911/17/comdex.elearning.idg/

Gottfredson, C and Mosher, B (2011) *Innovative Performance Support*, McGraw-Hill, New York

Logan, G (2007) [accessed 22 November 2016] The effects of 9/11 on the airline industry, *USA Today*, [Online] http://traveltips.usatoday.com/effects-911-airline-industry-63890.html

McCann, D (1999) [accessed 22 November 2016] Comdex Fall 99 in Las Vegas, *Classicmicro.com* [Online] http://www.classicmicro.com/comdex/1999/comdex99.htm

Old Computers (2016) [accessed 22 November 2016] Commodore PET, [Online] http://oldcomputers.net/pet2001.html

Schwartz, E (1999) [accessed 22 November 2016] Dick Tracy meets Star Trek, *CNN.com*, 16 November, [Online] http://edition.cnn.com/TECH/computing/9911/16/dick.tracy.star.trek/index.html

Sykes, R (1999) [accessed 22 November 2016] Comdex: Linux, Linux everywhere, *CNN.com*, 19 November, [Online] http://edition.cnn.com/TECH/computing/9911/19/comdex.linux.idg/index.html

Vasko, T (1986) [accessed 22 November 2016] Educational policies: an international overview, Working paper, [Online] http://webarchive.iiasa.ac.at/Admin/PUB/Documents/WP-86-052.pdf

Wikipedia (2016a) [accessed 22 November 2016] BBC Micro, [Online] https://en.wikipedia.org/wiki/BBC_Micro

Wikipedia (2016b) [accessed 22 November 2016] Dot-com bubble, [Online] https://en.wikipedia.org/wiki/Dot-com_bubble

How we learn at work   03

Good rules may do much, but good models far more; for in the latter we have instruction in action—wisdom at work. SAMUEL SMILES, BIOGRAPHER OF BOULTON AND WATT, 1865

In the previous chapter we saw how enthusiasts often overestimate how quickly technology will have an impact on learning. This has happened for any new technology capable of storing and/or transmitting information – from the phonograph to the radio to the long-playing record. When the ultimate information-sharing technology – the world wide web – was invented, it was predictable that once again enthusiasts would see it immediately transforming learning. The problem was that the enthusiasts imagined learning to be a matter of parcelling up information and doling it out. It is not, as we shall see. Further, most people in an organization laboured (and still labour) under the schoolroom assumption, by which all learning must take place in a course, and preferably in a classroom. Both these mindsets restricted the initial implementation of learning technologies – and continue to do so. They ignore the reality of how we actually learn at work, something we will explore in detail in this chapter, beginning with the very first people to attempt systematic training in the industrial age.

When engineering pioneers Matthew Boulton and James Watt began making some of the world's first truly effective steam engines in the late 18th century, they were breaking new ground. Not only were they inventing the machines themselves, they were creating the tools to build those machines. On top of that, they were developing the skilled workforce needed to create these machines from an assembly of workers with no experience of heavy industry, and precious little of working with power beyond that provided by human or animal muscles.

Based in Soho, just north of Birmingham, England, Boulton and Watt's works were able to draw on a base of highly talented local artisans who had developed their skills working at establishments in the forefront of the Industrial Revolution, such as Josiah Wedgwood's ceramics factories. Dextrous as the men were, they were generally new to mechanics and to engineering, and so Boulton and Watt developed a system to develop them to the required level. First, they provided basic instruction on the general nature of their work, followed by specialization in one particular area. As their biographer Samuel Smiles puts it: '[They would]… confine their workmen to special classes of work, and make them as expert in them as possible. By continued practice in handling the same tools and fabricating the same articles, they thus acquired great individual proficiency. "Without our tools and our workmen," said Watt, "very little could be done".' (Smiles, 1865)

Before long, Smiles notes, 'Soho was spoken of with pride as one of the best schools of skilled industry in England'. He also notes that Boulton and Watt suffered from the enduring issue of competitive firms in England and on the continent trying to poach these highly developed mechanics and engineers. More than 200 years before commentators were talking about intangible value, Boulton and Watt were gaining considerable competitive advantage by accumulating their human capital. And they were doing it by developing their workforce on the job, not in the classroom.

Informal learning

By developing skills on the job, these pioneers of the industrial age were doing what employees have been doing ever since, and what people have always done. They were learning from each other. In Learning and Development (L&D) terms, we call this learning informal, in contrast to learning by the sort of course-based formal instruction that will only develop skills up to a point.

Employees who learn from their own experience, and from the experience of those around them, are engaged in what Jay Cross, author of *Informal Learning*, described on his website, informl.com, as 'the unofficial, unscheduled, impromptu way most people learn to do their jobs'.

Jay estimated that 80 per cent of learning in the workplace is informal, the remainder formal, although he also pointed out that 'all learning is part formal and part informal' (Cross, 2012), a point also made in the seminal 1998 report *The Teaching Firm*, by the Education Development Center in Boston. This two-year study conducted extensive shadowing and observing, individual interviews, focus groups and surveys across seven major employers including Siemens, Ford and Boeing. The report points out that informal and formal learning feed off and reinforce each other. This makes it difficult to label any one particular piece of learning as being purely formal or informal (Aring and Brand, 1998).

The apprentice mechanics in Boulton and Watt's Soho factory were given some formal instruction at the beginning of their employment, and then during it as required. During the course of their work, of course, they also developed a deep specialism in whatever manual task they were engaged in, expanding on what they had been taught. When engaged in subsequent instruction, they would bring what they knew with them and share it – just as the Education Development Center noted, formal and informal learning were feeding off each other.

70:20:10

While people may argue over the precise definitions of informal and formal learning, and whether they are split 80 per cent informal to 20 per cent formal, or divided in some other way, nobody in the field of workplace learning denies they both exist, and most would agree that informal learning contributes more to our knowledge and actions than formal learning.

The 70:20:10 framework is another perspective on the different ways of learning at work. Most of what we learn comes to us via experience, a smaller part from other people, and the minority from structured courses and programmes.

The leading proponent of the 70:20:10 framework, Charles Jennings, is at pains to point out that it is a framework for thinking and action, rather than a rigid model, and that, in Charles's words, 'It's not about the Numbers, it's all about Change'. To Charles:

> The numbers are a useful reminder that most learning occurs in the context of the workplace rather than in formal learning situations and that learning is highly context dependent. The numbers provide a framework to support learning as it happens through challenging experiences, plenty of practice, rich conversations and the opportunity to reflect on what worked well and what didn't. (Jennings, 2012)

A lot of useless energy has been expended by L&D professionals obsessing on whether, in fact, 70 per cent of our learning is experiential, 20 per cent collaborative and 10 per cent formal. It is almost certainly a futile debate because it is impossible to definitively separate them as activities, and to ascribe any learning wholly to one and only one of these activities. At the risk of sounding like a broken record, these ways of learning are interdependent, as the Education Development Center study established. The point of the 70:20:10 framework is to establish in the minds of L&D professionals that the work they usually focus on most – formal delivery – is only one part of a large range of ways that people learn.

This is not to say that because formal instruction drives a minority of our learning, it is inconsequential. A building's foundations are always shorter than the building itself, and remain hidden, but without them the building will never last. In many cases, formal delivery is a vital constituent of the learning process, even if it takes up a minority of the learner's time and effort.

Formal programmes, however, need not necessarily be confined to a live class delivered in a physical classroom. Technology provides us ways of delivering formal programmes that only partially reflect the schoolroom assumption. The best of these combine the delivery of learning content with opportunities for safe practice, group work and experiential learning.

Blended learning

When it was originally coined in the 1990s, the term 'blended learning' was a misnomer. It was a way of incorporating the new ways of learning via electronic media into organizational learning programmes. In reality, 'blended learning' was synonymous with 'blended training delivery'. This blended delivery usually took the form of an 'e-learning sandwich' in which classroom activity was prefaced with some online pre-work, and followed up by online work for reinforcement and consolidation.

Since about 2010, however, 'blended learning' has moved away from focusing on delivery, and is now usually used to describe – like 70:20:10 – the ways in which the work of L&D professionals can support learning in the workplace. Of course, learning in the workplace is always blended, in the sense that we learn from a range of sources and activities, and in a variety of ways, over time, so really 'blended learning' should be synonymous with 'learning at work'. The term, however, serves a useful purpose in reminding L&D professionals that learning is about more than simply delivering information. It is also about practice, reflection, and – in particular – about fitting knowledge and skills to their work context.

Clive Shepherd acknowledges this past focus on delivery while emphasizing the need for workplace application clearly in the introduction to *More Than Blended Learning*:

> Blends are more efficient because they do not focus on a single delivery channel (such as the bricks-and-mortar classroom)... Blends, at least that those employ the *more than* approach, are also more effective, because they emphasise practical application and follow-through. (Shepherd, 2015)

Continuous learning

Proposed by David Mallon and Dani Johnson of Bersin by Deloitte, 'continuous learning' is similar to the above approaches in reflecting the complex way adults learn in the workplace. However, it explicitly aims to shift L&D's perception of itself from being providers of programmes and to focus on business priorities and the learner experience. In so doing, it sets itself a grand remit. Mallon and Johnson define continuous learning as: '… structuring resources, expectations, and learning culture in such a way as to encourage employees to learn continuously throughout their tenure with the organization.' (Johnson, 2014)

The model focuses on four Es: Education, Experience, Exposure and Environment, but the key emphasis is around the approach taken to foster learning in an organization. It should not be based on the materials that the L&D department produces, but instead should focus on expectations for holistic individual development, between 'stakeholders, including L&D, line management, learners themselves, and the organization as a whole' (Johnson, 2014).

The emphasis on the cultural aspects of learning is particularly important in this model, as Johnson makes clear: 'While L&D should take responsibility for overall organizational learning, this does not mean they must execute everything by themselves. They should seek input from several functions and coordinate with other groups in order to make these changes happen.'

So how do we learn at work?

Adult learning is a complex business, and it should be no surprise that there are many different ways of describing how it happens at work, and the role of the L&D department in supporting it. It was not always so. Once we were content to follow a simpler, classroom-based model, but a faster business environment, learning technologies, and (as we shall see) the increased importance of organizational human capital have precipitated a rich vein of thinking and debate in this field.

The brief mention of these models here can only scratch the surface of the vibrant discussion underway in contemporary thinking about the best ways of supporting workplace learning. Bob Mosher and Conrad Gottfredson's work on performance, mentioned earlier, is another crucial component of modern thinking about learning at work. So, too, is the work of Nigel Harrison on Performance Consulting, which we will examine when we look at the all-important initial stages of a successful learning technology implementation.

The models mentioned here all differ in tone and application, but linking them are two common themes that are crucial to this book. The first is that – whichever model you take as your guide – adult learning is a complex, multifaceted thing, made even more complex by the power structures and competing demands of a modern workplace. Although it is difficult – in fact, precisely because it is difficult – it is incumbent on L&D professionals to steep themselves in a profound understanding of the science behind adult learning. It is our job. If we do not take the time to take it seriously, nobody else will, and the business will fall back on whoever is selling the latest fad in this field to meet their needs.

The second theme is that technology changes everything. Clive Shepherd is right to say that 'technology is an important enabler here, providing opportunities that we could have only dreamed about 20 years ago,' but that is only one side of the coin. Technology is both an important enabler and an unrelenting taskmaster. It makes much possible, but also sets a pace of business that demands employees know more, faster – often at a pace that seems to make learning impossible (Shepherd, 2015).

Over 200 years ago, Matthew Boulton and James Watt faced problems of skilling up a workforce, problems which were almost entirely new. Now, after the Industrial Revolution, which they set in motion, we are in a similar position. We are in a new world of work, less hierarchical, more fluid, more interconnected and working at a faster pace than Boulton and Watt's factories and their successors ever did. Human capital is more important than ever today, and the Learning and Development function plays a vital part in building it. The only way it can do that effectively and keep pace with the modern world is by using a range of learning technologies.

Key takeaways

1 The schoolroom assumption – that learning relies on courses and being taught – runs counter to research into how adults learn in the workplace.

2 Much of our learning as adults in the workplace is informal, although it is difficult to define where the impact of informal learning ends and that of formal learning begins.

3 The 70:20:10 model says that adult learning is a mixture of experiential, collaborative and formal learning, although not necessarily in those precise proportions.

4 Modern blended learning emphasizes multiple delivery channels as well as practical application and follow-through after any learning intervention.

5 Continuous learning centres on the need for L&D to focus on business priorities and the learner experience rather than on delivering training programmes.

6 As well as these models of learning, L&D professionals use models of performance support (Gottfredson and Mosher) and performance consulting (Harrison).

References

Aring, M and Brand, B (1998) [accessed 22 November 2016] *The Teaching Firm: Where productive work and learning converge*, report on research findings and implications, Education Development Center, Inc., Newton, MA, [Online] http://files.eric.ed.gov/fulltext/ED461754.pdf

Cross, J (2012) [accessed 22 November 2016] Where did the 80% come from? [Online] www.informl.com/where-did-the-80-come-from/

Jennings, C (2012) [accessed 22 November 2016] 70:20:10 – It's not about the numbers, it's all about change, *Charles Jennings Workplace Performance*, 6 June, [Online] http://charles-jennings.blogspot.co.uk/2012/06/702010-its-not-about-numbers-its-all.html

Johnson, D (2014) [accessed 22 November 2016] Getting From 70:20:10 to Continuous Learning, *Bersin by Deloitte Research Bulletin*, December, [Online] https://www2.deloitte.com/content/dam/Deloitte/at/Documents/human-capital/research-bulletin-2014.pdf

Shepherd, C (2015) *More Than Blended Learning*, Lulu.com, Raleigh, NC

Smiles, S (1865) *The Lives of Boulton and Watt*, John Murray, London, [Online] www.gutenberg.org/files/52069/52069-h/52069-h.htm [accessed 22 November 2016]

What are learning technologies and why bother with them?

04

Technology is... 'stuff that doesn't work yet'. BRAN FERREN,
QUOTED BY DOUGLAS ADAMS (ADAMS, 1999)

Previously we have looked at how we learn at work, together with some of the history of e-learning and learning technologies and one of the key factors holding back their adoption – the schoolroom assumption. It's now time to explore the extent to which organizations are turning to learning technologies, and the drivers behind adoption. In order to do that, we will need to define both 'e-learning' and 'learning technologies'.

What are 'learning technologies'?

If we are to implement a 'learning technology' in the workplace, just what are we implementing? It's a fair question to ask, but one that is difficult to answer precisely. The human instinct to learn is so fundamental that we will use any technology at hand to help us. A book is a powerful learning technology. So are a pencil and notepad. The radio or television can be a source of entertainment one moment and a learning technology the next, and, of course, we can both learn and be entertained at the same time.

In short, almost anything manufactured can be described as a learning technology. This is not, however, a very useful definition for a book about implementing learning technologies, neither does it chime with what most people would understand by the phrase – something new, something electronic, probably something using the internet a lot of the time, something like 'e-learning'. Indeed, if we are to narrow down the definition of learning technology for this book, it makes sense to focus on what exactly we mean by 'e-learning'.

As with the term 'learning technology', there has been plenty of debate about the definition of 'e-learning', but for me Clive Shepherd has the answer. Clive, based in the UK, has been in the field of learning since the early 1980s, and in *The Really Useful eLearning Instruction Manual* (Hubbard, 2013) he puts forward this definition of e-learning: 'When we use computers and the networks to which these are linked, to in some way support the learning process.'

This is commendably broad, is not tied to any particular technology beyond computers and networks, and describes e-learning in terms of 'supporting the learning process'. This makes it explicit that learning is a human activity, something too often forgotten by many learning technologists who slip into talking about 'delivering learning', as if people were passive consumers of information – harking back to the phonograph and radio and the misguided belief that learning can be transformed solely by a technology that packages content and delivers it.

In addition to the definition, Clive suggests that there are five different types of e-learning:

- Self-study lessons – also known as traditional e-learning, these are where an individual learns, alone, from pre-prepared materials, usually in a course format. This is where the infamous instruction to 'click next' has too often been used ('next' being the wording on the on-screen button to be pressed to move to the next screen). This is where e-learning gets its reputation for leading people down a boring, linear path with no interaction and little meaning. E-learning self-study need not be like this, but too often is.

- Virtual classrooms – often overlooked as a learning technology because they have become very much part of our lives through online meetings. In their most basic form they present a very familiar experience: a person talks, shows slides, and people listen. Even with this basic format, the advantages are clear: travel is reduced and people can attend for shorter periods than they would a regular class. Of course, talking at people online can be as boring as asking people to repeatedly click a button, just as a classroom class will be tedious or enthralling, depending on the trainer. Too often the medium carries the blame for the sins of the practitioner.

- Simulations and virtual worlds – done well, these can be incredibly engaging, and a great vehicle for learning. While simulations do not require technology (effective paper-based simulations have been run for years), they definitely benefit from the immediate feedback that technology allows. With the arrival of cost-effective virtual and augmented reality technology platforms, this is a coming technology, as we shall see in Part Three.

- Online resources – when people say they don't like 'e-learning', this usually means that they don't like traditional self-study lessons. They seldom consider that looking up something on Google, YouTube or Wikipedia is e-learning, but of course it often is. The same applies to using resources created during work by those inside an organization and those in communities outside. A wise approach to workplace learning will harness all these materials as part of constructing an overall learning environment.

- Online collaboration – one of the most natural ways of learning is to ask someone a question such as 'What does this mean?' or 'How do I do this?' Online collaboration tools allow us to do this in ways undreamed of only a decade ago. This makes these tools ideal for just-in-time learning, which solves a problem on the spot. In addition, though, prolonged online collaboration develops individuals' just-in-case capability, too. As they explore topics through online discussion, they come to a better understanding of them, ready to put that understanding to use when required.

Clive's broad definition, with its five subcategories, is an excellent, comprehensive definition of e-learning. We will base our definition of 'learning technology' on it. For the purposes of this book, we will restrict our definition of 'learning technology' to the very narrow sense of 'anything used to support e-learning'.

This approach also makes it clear that we live and work in a complex ecosystem of learning technologies, where e-learning is not the sole province of courses, and access to learning materials is not solely achieved through a Learning Management System (LMS), but through a range of media.

Wherever we work, we are likely to use more than one technology for learning (whether we do so consciously or not) and many of these systems will not necessarily be owned or even controlled by our employers. In contrast to the 'command and control' that John Chambers alluded to in his 1999 COMDEX speech, increasingly the tools we use for learning are part of the general environment in which we live. Tools such as Google and YouTube are used daily to look up facts and to learn new skills at home as much as at work. While we may not need to implement these technologies in the sense of making them work technically, we certainly do need to facilitate their use in the sense of making them work to meet our desired learning outcomes. They are all part of our complex learning technology ecosystem.

The demand for learning technologies

As we saw in the previous chapter, there was a strong cost-cutting motive for investing in learning technologies in the late 1990s, which accelerated after the 9/11 terrorist attacks. Compounded by a misunderstanding of the nature of learning – that it consists only of packaging up and delivering information – this led to a proliferation of unimaginative courses, driven by the mistaken assumption that it is possible to somehow put the slides from a face-to-face course online and for the result to be as effective as it is in the classroom.

This style of training is ineffective for helping people learn, it is boring to sit through, and it seldom changes behaviour. Its continued use in L&D is down to two things. First, in industries where compliance training requires no more than employees attending a course (regardless of whether they learn anything or alter their actions subsequently), this method of training is the cheapest way to push people through a process and track it.

The second driver is the balance of power between those commissioning training programmes (typically those in operational management) and those executing them (typically the training or L&D department). Too often the managers have the power and the L&D department lacks either the clout or the negotiating skills to demand a more effective approach to delivery. Sadly, it is also the case that sometimes the L&D department lacks the ability and insight to deliver anything beyond a knowledge dump masquerading as training.

If learning technologies resulted only in the production of 'click next' training for inadequate compliance courses, they would be nothing more than a side bar in organizational arrangements. They are very far from that.

Used well, learning technologies provide real value for the organizations that use them – value that we will explore in Chapter 9, when we explore the various reasons learning technologies are implemented. To understand that corporations appreciate that value, one need look no further than the marketplace. In 2014, Bersin by Deloitte estimated the 2014 global corporate market for Learning Management Systems (LMSs) to be worth US $2.5 billion, up from an estimated US $1.9 billion the year before (Bersin, 2014). In 2015, Capterra estimated the corporate market to be worth US $2.5 billion, with the combined corporate and educational reckoned to be US $7.8 billion by 2018 (Medved, 2015).

LMSs are not the only learning technology, but they are a type that is relatively easy to define and assign a value to, in contrast to the plethora of systems that straddle training and other areas, such as HR or internal communications. If we assume the LMS market is not peculiar in some way, and is a fair indicator of the general sentiment in this area, it is clear that organizations are prepared to pay substantially for learning technologies, and to pay in increasing amounts each year. It looks as if organizations are finding value well beyond simply saving some of the cost of classroom training.

What are these organizations paying for? That depends on the technology they are buying.

According to Capterra's survey, the LMS is still largely used in the corporate space for internal skills and certification training (roughly 60 per cent of respondents) with 30 to 40 per cent of respondents using the LMS for compliance and onboarding training. This might be what you would expect from a system that is usually bought to complement or replace formal, face-to-face training. However, the list of 'Most desired features' on the same survey shows that the ambitions of corporate LMS buyers go beyond simply replacing the classroom experience. They include live/video conferencing (38 per cent), mobile learning (27 per cent) and social learning (20 per cent).

These numbers show a substantial minority of LMS buyers are looking for something beyond replicating a traditional learning experience. And this in a tool that is usually seen precisely as enabling an online replication of classroom training. Given the overall rising sales of learning technologies (11 per cent annual growth to US $31billion internationally by 2020), clearly organizations are undergoing a shift in their approach to training and learning (Technavio, 2016).

This is a fundamental point. Organizations are buying learning technologies because they hope to meet learning needs in a way that traditional training delivery cannot. This despite the fact that until relatively recently (around 2000), traditional classroom delivery was considered perfectly adequate for all learning needs. This new approach to organizational learning is driven by some deep changes taking place in how we work, in the nature of organizations and in the economy itself.

The drivers for adopting learning technologies

The world of work today is very different from what it was 20 or even 10 years ago. We are now experiencing the results of changes triggered decades ago simultaneously coming to fruition. The result is three drivers for organizations to adopt learning technologies.

The first driver – the changing nature of our economy – began making its impact felt before the Second World War. Since then all developed economies have shifted away from manufacturing as the major contributor to Gross Domestic Product (GDP). Services now make up over 75 per cent of the UK and US economies (World Bank, 2014). With that shift has come a change in what constitutes the value of an organization. When manufacturing dominated, that value could be measured in terms of tangible assets: plant, property, stocks and so on. In service industries, value is reckoned mostly in terms of intangible assets. Erik Brynjolfsson and Andrew McAfee divide these into four types: intellectual property, organizational capital, user-generated content and human capital (Brynjolfsson and McAfee, 2014).

The increase in the importance of intangible assets has been tracked by Ocean Tomo, looking at the value of companies in the S&P 500 Index. In the 1970s, 20 per cent of their value would typically be intangible. Today it is usually 80 per cent or above (Ocean Tomo, 2013). From being a small part of an organization's worth in the 1970s, human capital is now an essential component, described by Brynjolfsson and McAfee as the most important of their four types of intangible value.

When people play that large a role in an organization's value, maintaining and growing their skills and knowledge become crucial. In addition it becomes essential to ensure two of the other types of intangible value are best exploited – intellectual property and user-generated content – by sharing them rapidly around the organization. While it is unlikely that the C-suite is investing in learning technologies explicitly for these reasons, organizations are certainly buying systems that help them address their symptoms. Black & Decker (now Stanley Black & Decker) gave 250 field sales people in the United States Flip cameras and asked them to record short videos of how they sold power tools, and how to pitch against particular competitive products (Albright *et al*, 2011). The videos were uploaded and shared across the team using an LMS. In L&D, we would call that user-generated content supporting staff knowledge and performance at the point of need. The business would call it finding a way to sell better.

This reliance on human beings as the differentiators between organizations is only going to continue as jobs are increasingly automated. The roles that remain will either be location based, or highly skilled and/or creative. That, at least, is the prediction of Frey and Osborne of Oxford University, whose 2013 paper 'The Future of Employment' foresees that within the next 10 to 20 years 47 per cent of US jobs are at risk of what they call 'computerization', that is, being taken over by machines or algorithms (Frey and Osborne, 2013). Machines and algorithms can be copied at scale. People can't. In the future, the importance of human capital as a differentiator between organizations, and the source of competitive edge, will be even more acutely felt.

Automation doesn't happen suddenly, with a robot invasion. It insidiously creeps into our lives, as those with automatable skills silently disappear. When a major UK law firm moved into its new HQ in the up-and-coming Docklands district of London in 2000, it had a fax machine on every floor. Sitting by each machine was a 'fax lady', whose sole job was to collect and distribute faxes when they arrived, and, in turn, to send off faxes and to ensure confirmation of delivery. It was not many years before e-mail use rendered the need for fax machines redundant and slowly, one by one, the 'fax ladies' disappeared. The more highly skilled lawyers, however, remain, providing the human skills of creativity, synthesis, sense-making and pattern-forming demanded in the highly automated service economy.

If the nature of the economy has changed, and with it, the nature of work, so too have organizations, and this is the second driver behind the adoption of learning technologies. Increasingly the hierarchical organization of the past is changing into something looser and more distributed. Increasingly companies outsource, working in partnership and relying on people outside the organization, whether they are in joint ventures, in supply or distribution chains, and whether they work as contractors, freelancers or something else. By 2020, Deloitte calculates that 50 per cent of the people a company relies on will not be on the payroll (Schwartz, 2013). If you have ever run a learning programme and struggled to get everyone to attend when they are all full-time employees, working on a single site, you will appreciate that reaching people off-site, often working in different countries, possibly in unpredictable shift patterns, and usually with a very weak affiliation to the company, is a whole new challenge for L&D.

The third driver is simple: things just happen faster today. Product cycles are shorter, and adoption curves faster. In 2013, *Harvard Business Review* reported that a typical automotive design cycle was 24 to 36 months, against the 60-month cycle of five years earlier (McGrath, 2013). The same article points out that it took decades for the telephone to reach 50 per cent of US households, while achieving the same penetration for mobile phones took just five years. The result is a more pressured environment for businesses. Investors who once took a long-term view are now impatient for returns, and unwilling to forgive short-term setbacks. In the 1960s, stocks in US companies were held for an average of over eight years. Today that average is under six months. This all makes it harder to stay at the top (Ro, 2012). In 1958, the average company in the S&P 500 Index remained there for 61 years. Today, the average company can expect to stay no longer than 20 years (Basenese, 2014).

This relentless demand for speed affects us all, L&D included. When timescales for project completion are shortened and product cycles truncated, and while businesses operate in an increasingly competitive environment, it is essential people are ready for work, fully skilled, with access to the information and advice they need to perform effectively.

These three factors will be familiar to anyone working today: the increased importance of people to organizations in a highly automated, service economy demanding truly effective learning, the increasingly distributed nature of modern organizations, and the increased speed of work today. To succeed today, organizations must be effective, scalable and fast, and L&D must be too.

Could L&D not meet these changes using traditional classroom training delivery? The answer is simple: almost certainly not. Face-to-face classroom interaction is excellent for certain types of learning, for example when people feel particularly vulnerable, or when they need to model complex human behaviours. Beyond those instances, however, classroom training is not particularly effective, and it is certainly neither scalable nor fast. Learning technologies, by contrast, can scale, are fast enough to do this, and – crucially – are affordable, which large-scale classroom training is not. Most modern organizations simply cannot learn well enough, fast enough and widely enough, by relying on classroom training.

But are learning technologies effective? To give an equivocal answer, the answer is yes, they are effective if – like any medium – they are used well.

Using the classroom to transfer information is terribly inefficient. In the past, when all we had were people, books and physical space, it was the best tool available. And yet studies have repeatedly shown that retention of new facts learned in isolation from application – which is what usually happens in a classroom – is notoriously low. The most often cited research is Herman Ebbinghaus's studies into memorizing groups of nonsense syllables. The resulting 'Forgetting Curve' demonstrates a rapid decline in the ability to recall information. A better approach is spaced learning, where people learn a small amount of information in one go, and are reminded of it over regular intervals. In his extensive review of spaced learning, Dr Will Thalheimer points out that over 300 studies in the 20th century have confirmed the value of learning spaced out over time (Thalheimer, 2006). While it is possible to do this in a classroom – perhaps using sessions of a few minutes – this is a poor use of time, especially given the need to travel to the classroom. Learning technologies, in contrast, are very well suited to delivering reminders of information learned, or nudges to work in a particular way.

Spaced learning helps when there is a clear body of material to be covered – a curriculum, if you will. Learning technologies are a very effective way to deliver this, when used well. They are also useful, though, in areas where learning is less formal. People learn in many other ways. Mostly through self-directed enquiry, using people or other resources to gather what they need. Learning technologies are particularly suited to making these available at the moment when people need them – often moments 3, 4 and 5 in Mosher and Gottfredson's five moments of learning need that we saw earlier:

3 When they need to act upon what they have learned (Apply).

4 When problems arise (Solve).

5 When people need to learn a new way of doing something, which requires them to change skills and ingrained practices (Change).

As well as making people and resources available, of course, learning technologies can also be used to curate them, and to source them from fellow employees. When intangible assets are so important, this sharing of intellectual property and user-generated content (to use Brynjolfsson and McAfee's terms) at speed, across today's widely distributed organizations, makes a compelling case for learning technologies.

Substitution or addition?

The great power of the web, and the speed of change we live in today, make it easy to be an unthinking cheerleader for learning technologies. In particular, it is easy to imagine that learning technologies are a simple replacement for classroom training. That would be a mistake.

Replacement technologies – where an existing tool or method can be switched out and replaced with a new one – have a particular, often dramatic impact. According to the consulting company Bain, music CD sales in the United States peaked at US $15 billion of value around the year 2000 (Béhar *et al*, 2010). Within nine years, they had slumped to US $5 billion. By 2015, US sales had slumped to US $1.5 billion, putting CD sales just below revenues generated from streaming services such as Spotify, a fall of 84 per cent in a decade (Sisario and Russellmarch, 2016).

Classroom training has not undergone such a dramatic slump. It still constitutes the largest part of the L&D mix in most organizations. According to the UK's Learning and Performance Institute's 2015 Learning Survey, over 50 per cent of approximately 500 respondents said classroom training made up the largest part of their work (LPI, 2015a).

Why has classroom training proved so resilient, in the face of the drivers demanding organizations and L&D be effective, scalable and fast?

One reason is the very human tendency to tackle any problem with the tool that is most familiar, regardless of whether it is necessarily the best. The tool most familiar to the L&D profession is the physical classroom. In the same LPI survey, classroom training certificates were by far the most commonly held qualifications of respondents (43 per cent had some qualification). In addition, of 27 skills for the L&D profession identified on the LPI's Capability Map, one skill stands out as the most commonly held. In the March 2015 cut of data, over 90 per cent of nearly 2,000 people taking the self-assessment said they were skilled in *Presentation Delivery*. And respondents rated themselves highly at it, with an average level of expertise of 3.26 out of 4, the second highest level of all the 27 skills. The L&D profession's skillset is, currently, firmly rooted in the classroom (LPI, 2015b).

Another reason lies outside L&D, among the employees, managers and executives of the organizations they serve. As noted earlier, the schoolroom assumption casts a powerful influence over how we think we should learn, and exerts a strong cultural lag on any attempts to change approaches to learning. We should not underestimate the strength of this common cultural bond, nor its power to restrain any attempts to change the status quo.

The final reason, however, cannot be ignored. Sometimes a physical space *is* the best place for a learning activity, be it a formal course or less formal practice, role-play or collaboration. Learning technology is not a straightforward replacement for the classroom. Used well, it extends our ability to learn beyond anything we would do in the classroom, in the ways that are most natural to us – by asking questions and seeking out information. Because this is revolutionary, and quite unlike the entire history of formalized learning and training, we are still learning how to make best use of the learning technologies available to us.

This chapter has set the background for Part Two of this book, which is as much about changing people's learning habits as it is about implementing technology. Before we can start Part Two, however, there are two more things to consider: the different types of learning technologies, and before that, something that has long been the core of L&D's role: the material that people learn from.

Key takeaways

1 This book uses Clive Shepherd's definition of e-learning: 'When we use computers and the networks to which these are linked, to in some way support the learning process.'

2 We also use a narrow definition of learning technologies: 'anything used to support e-learning'.

3 The demands for learning technologies is high and increasing, with the global corporate market for just one technology – the LMS – estimated in the billions of US dollars.

4 There is evidence that organizations are looking for learning technologies not merely to replace the classroom experience, but to add to it and extend it.

5 There are three drivers for this increased demand for learning technologies. The first is the increased importance of people and their knowledge in a service economy.

6 The second driver is that work is becoming increasingly distributed across employees and non-employees, and across different geographical locations.

7 The third driver is the increased speed of business today, demanding a rapid response to changes, and the ability to communication new information fast.

8 In general, learning technologies meet the demands of this new environment better than traditional classroom training because of their flexibility, and because they make it easy to deliver content spaced over time.

9 Learning technologies are also particularly useful for sharing information and connecting people in ways that event-driven courses cannot. They help people learn across all of the moments of need identified by Mosher and Gottfredson.

10 Classroom training has not slumped with the advent of learning technologies. One reason is the schoolroom assumption and the resistance to change it induces, but another is that sometimes the classroom *is* the best place to learn.

References

Adams, D (1999) [accessed 24 November 2016] How to Stop Worrying and Learn to Love the Internet, *Sunday Times*, 29 August, [Online] www.douglasadams.com/dna/19990901-00-a.html

Albright, S, Bailey, M and Walker, D (2011) [accessed 25 November 2016] Next Learning Unwrapped. Chapter 5: Learn-on-the-Go-Podcasts, *Videocasts and Mobile Learning*, pp 27–31, [Online] https://issuu.com/elearningevent/docs/chapter_5_next_learning

Basenese, L (2014) [accessed 25 November 2016] 375 Companies Prepare for the Guillotine, *Wall Street Daily*, 31 January, [Online] www.wallstreetdaily.com/2014/01/31/creative-destruction-sp/

Béhar, P, Colombani, L and Krishnan, S (2010) [accessed 25 November 2016] Publishing in the Digital Era, *Bain and Company*, 20 October, [Online] www.bain.com/publications/articles/publishing-in-digital-era.aspx

Bersin, J (2014) Learning Management Systems 2014: Making the right decision to support high-impact learning, *Bersin by Deloitte*, Oakland, California

Brynjolfsson, E and McAfee, A (2014) *The Second Machine Age: Work, progress, and prosperity in a time of brilliant technologies*, W W Norton & Company, New York

Frey, C and Osborne, M (2013) [accessed 25 November 2016] The Future of Employment: How susceptible are jobs to computerisation? *University of Oxford: Oxford Martin School*, [Online] www.oxfordmartin.ox.ac.uk/downloads/academic/The_Future_of_Employment.pdf

Hubbard, R (2013) *The Really Useful eLearning Instruction Manual*, Wiley, Chichester

LPI (2015a) [accessed 25 November 2016] The Learning Survey 2015, *Learning and Performance Institute*, Coventry, [Online] https://www.thelpi.org/data-papers-press/learning-survey-2015/

LPI (2015b) The LPI Capability Map, 2015 Report [Unpublished report]

McGrath, R (2013) [accessed 25 November 2016] The Pace of Technology Adoption is Speeding Up, *Harvard Business Review*, 25 November, [Online] https://hbr.org/2013/11/the-pace-of-technology-adoption-is-speeding-up

Medved, J P, (2015) [accessed 24 November 2016] LMS Industry User Research Report, *Capterra*, 8 April, [Online] www.capterra.com/learning-management-system-software/user-research

Ocean Tomo (2013) [accessed 25 November 2016] Ocean Tomo's Intangible Asset Market Value Study, *Ocean Tomo*, 12 September, [Online] www.oceantomo.com/2013/12/09/Intangible-Asset-Market-Value-Study-Release/

Ro, S (2012) [accessed 25 November 2016] Stock Market Investors Have Become Absurdly Impatient, *Business Insider*, 7 August, [Online] www.businessinsider.com/stock-investor-holding-period-2012-8?IR=T

Schwartz, J (2013) [accessed 25 November 2016] Resetting Horizons: Global human capital trends 2013, *Deloitte*, [Online] https://www2.deloitte.com/content/dam/Deloitte/global/Documents/HumanCapital/dttl-humancapital-trends6-open-talent-next-no-exp.pdf

Sisario, B and Russellmarch, K (2016) [accessed 25 November 2016] In Shift to Streaming, Music Business Has Lost Billions, *New York Times*, 24 March, [Online] www.nytimes.com/2016/03/25/business/media/music-sales-remain-steady-but-lucrative-cd-sales-decline.html?_r=0

Technavio (2016) [accessed 25 November 2016] Global Corporate E-learning Market to Reach over USD 31 Billion by 2020, says Technavio, *Business Wire*, [Online] www.businesswire.com/news/home/20160129005032/en/Global-Corporate-E-learning-Market-Reach-USD-31

Thalheimer, W (2006) [accessed 25 November 2016] Spacing Learning Over Time, *Work-Learning Research Inc.*, [Online] http://willthalheimer.typepad.com/files/spacing_learning_over_time_2006.pdf

World Bank (2014) [accessed 24 November 2016] World Development Indicators: Structure of output, *World Bank*, [Online] http://wdi.worldbank.org/table/4.2

Platforms, content and communication

05

Conversation is the most powerful learning technology ever invented. JAY CROSS

Having spent some time defining learning technologies in the last chapter, we now go on to look at how those learning technologies can be categorized. This is a thankless task: it can never be completed, because new learning technologies evolve all the time. In addition, it is unbounded, because every technology can be used for learning. Any list of types of learning technologies must, therefore, be both out of date and incomplete.

The root cause of this lies not in our technologies, but in ourselves. We are learning animals. This is not a metaphor, it is the literal truth, and it is a truth core to our success as a species. From the starting point of an African exodus some 100,000–70,000 years ago, we now – for better or worse – populate and dominate every corner of our planet. We were able to accomplish this because of our adaptability; no other species is as widely spread, successfully coping with such a range of local environments. And behind this success lie two secrets. First, we learn from experience and experimentation. Second, and as importantly, we are able, through the power of language, to communicate what we have learned across generations. Jay Cross was right when he said: 'Conversation is the most powerful learning technology ever invented'.

Humans are insatiable learners, always picking up something new and passing it on, and we have been doing it long before there were trainers, facilitators and learning technologists. Which is a problem for this book. If we can learn from anything, then in our hands any technology becomes a learning technology, and the scope of the book becomes impossibly large. This is not a trivial semantic point. There are plenty of technologies not explicitly designed to support learning that nonetheless are used very successfully to that end. The wide range of sharing tools – including platforms such as Twitter – are clear examples of tools used for learning and much else.

Then there are technologies that have been set up to cover a range of things, including learning. The most obvious is the printing press, but this also includes more modern platforms such as those for virtual reality and gaming.

In addition, there are technologies that are bent – successfully or otherwise – towards learning. Googling the phrase 'X for learning', where X is a fairly new technology, will always yield a result. Sometimes the attempt is fanciful – 'Drones for learning' yields about 10,000 results on Google – but QR codes, Pinterest and other technologies have been very successful when used for learning.

And then, of course, there are technologies that are produced explicitly with the intention of supporting adult learning in the workplace. These are mostly what this book is about, although it is inevitable that the most successful consumer platforms such as YouTube, and communications tools such as Yammer will be included too.

This is a very wide group of technologies. Is it worthwhile categorizing them? Is it even possible? Some have tried. Richard Culatta, former Director at the US Office of Educational Technology and current Chief Innovation Officer at the State of Rhode Island, has collected a range of useful ways of looking at learning technology (Culatta, 2011). One is to group them by function:

- Social tools
- Collaboration
- Broadcasting tools
- Media repositories
- Assessment and evaluation tools
- Real-time learning environments
- Asynchronous learning environments

This makes sense – we can immediately think of a tool and know which category it belongs to. A webinar platform, for example, would be an example of a broadcasting tool. A moment's reflection, however, might give us pause for thought. Such a platform can also be used for meetings, where people are brought together to discuss a common problem. That might make it also a social tool or a collaborative one or both. It seems that a technology can fit into more than category.

A simpler model is based on types of learning interactions. Suggested by learning theorist Michael G Moore, it was put forward in 1989, as technology was making its impact felt in learning (Moore, 1989), and was formulated as a way of understanding how people learn at a distance. It identifies three types of interaction:

- Learner–Content
- Learner–Instructor/Expert
- Learner–Learner

Learning technologies may be grouped according to how they connect the two participants in these interactions – they may connect learners with each other, or with experts, or with content. As with the previous categorization by function, a technology can, of course, encourage more than one type of interaction, but this way of looking at learning technology has the advantage of focusing on what we actually do with it (eg form connections) rather than what it claims to do (for example, broadcast or assess).

While Moore's three interactions have the strength of simplicity, perhaps inevitably people have sought to add to it. Culatta adds a fourth interaction: Learner–Context (Culatta, 2011). Earlier, in 1994, Hillman, Willis and Gunawardena suggested a similar kind of extra interaction: Student–Interface (Hillman *et al*, 1994). Any taxonomy will always be subject to additions and revisions, and with good reason; it is right always to question the ways we make sense of the world. For this book, however, I am happy to stick with Moore's original three groups. It is a simple, useful reminder that what matters about technologies is not their ostensible functionality, but rather what we use them for. YouTube was originally for sharing holiday videos, after all.

Putting the aim before the technology like this is not an academic exercise, it is part of the mindset of successful learning technologists. All tools have their own designed functionality, but when implementing them, we should always be driven by our learning and business goals, not by a technological promise.

This approach is also an attempt to avoid the pointless, but passionate argument that tends to accompany technology, an area where people take firmly entrenched sides very quickly. People become avid supporters of a technology, or dismissive detractors of it, in an instant. They loathe Microsoft PowerPoint, or they love it. (Well, at least one person once claimed to love PowerPoint (Porter, 2015).) Categorizing technologies by our intended use of them is a way around that. Technologies are neither inherently good nor bad. They are only either useful or not, and may be used well or poorly. Those that are useful are enthusiastically adopted, to the benefit of both employees and the business. Ideally, technologies that are not useful, or which are poorly implemented, would be rejected by employees and left unused. However, that is not what happens. Instead, employees are forced to use them, and that is what led to Sally's very understandable frustration in Starbucks, making her say 'I get that we have to do this, but why do they gotta make doing it so hard?'

Being forced to use inadequate learning technologies is one direct route to frustration for employees. Another is learning technologies that are oversold and which under-deliver. Too often technology enthusiasts push a platform or tool or medium to levels of expectation that they cannot possibly meet. In Part Two we will explore how to tackle this key issue of setting and managing expectations. Before that, however, I want to look at the first of Moore's categories in more detail, the link between learner and content. This is not to say that the other two categories are not important. Arguably, the technology that links learner to learner or learner to expert is more important as a way of supporting our natural ways of informal learning. However, most of the work in learning technology implementations currently is around platforms that share content, so these tools demand our attention.

Private content platforms

No discussion of learning technologies would be complete without considering the epitome of a content-managing technology: the learning management system, or LMS. As we saw in the previous chapter, billions of dollars are spent on LMSs globally. They are typically high-investment pieces of technology and an LMS deployment will likely be the most complex project an L&D department will ever be responsible for.

It is fair to say that opinion is divided on LMSs. They are frequently vilified by both the employees using the systems and the L&D departments running them. It is very likely that 'Sally', the anonymous employee whose tale of frustration began this book, was using an LMS. At the 2010 Learning Technologies Conference in London, in front of about 100 training professionals, a speaker asked: 'Who here can honestly say they love their LMS?' A solitary hand went up. The audience's reaction: consternation that even one hand was raised.

If no technology is inherently good or bad, what is it that makes so many people hate LMSs so violently? And why, despite this, do organizations spend so heavily on them?

Although modern LMSs do much more than just deliver courses, the LMS is still a content-focused technology. For large organizations in particular, buying one represents a good investment for managing the vast numbers of e-learning courses and other online resources that they have accumulated. And while an LMS is expensive, the direct and opportunity costs of classroom training are so high that if just some of this material can be distributed online rather than in a classroom, the LMS will usually more than justify its cost.

Cost-saving on delivery is not the most common driving factor for the purchase of LMSs, however. Most large organizations have some form of training that they need to deliver, track and report on. This could be mandatory compliance training, such as anti-money laundering training in UK and US banks, or it could be reporting on training delivery to meet government guidelines, as with training levies or the South African Broad-Based Black Economic Empowerment laws.

The pressure of this increasingly regulatory environment and the need to marshal learning resources means that 75 per cent of the 600 organizations surveyed in the 2016–17 Towards Maturity benchmark report have an LMS (Towards Maturity, 2016).

So, the LMS is often bought for administrative reasons rather than to provide learning that is effective, scalable and fast. This does not mean that purchasing one to meet these administrative reasons is wrong (from a business point of view it makes perfect sense) nor that the LMS cannot also be used for high-quality training. What it does mean – and this is crucial to gain high-level backing in any organization – is that before anything else, the LMS must be seen to be used effectively for this primary purpose, or it risks losing senior stakeholder support. Doing a good job with this primary purpose is also essential for keeping employee support; every compliance course, every piece of e-learning must be as engaging and effective as possible. It is the L&D department's shop window to the rest of the organization. Reducing it to the type of 'click next' self-study lessons that Sally was subjected to will not only alienate employees from the LMS, but from e-learning and possibly learning technologies in general.

There are many hard-learned lessons of successful LMS implementations, but this one underlines them all: however the decision to implement an LMS was arrived at, it is generally such a high-stakes investment, and its impact is so widely seen, that the fate of the L&D department depends on making a success of it.

A significant minority of LMS implementations are unpopular. According to Capterra's 2015 study, 26 per cent of respondents were either dissatisfied or very dissatisfied with their current LMS (63 per cent were satisfied or very satisfied). Of those who were dissatisfied, easily the largest single group (44 per cent) said it was because the system lacked certain features. Of those that had switched LMSs, nearly 70 per cent said they had done so because their previous LMS 'lacked the features needed' (Medved, 2015).

This is telling. If purchasing an LMS is a high-stakes investment, then why buy one lacking the required functionality? There are several possibilities, and each says something about our relationship with the LMS in particular, and with learning technologies in general.

It is possible that the purchasing decision was made without properly consulting the L&D department, or indeed it being consulted at all. This may happen because the department lacks sufficient influence. It is also possible that the organization has an existing legacy LMS which the organizational leadership is not prepared to replace – although this again amounts to the L&D department having insufficient influence. After all, if the LMS does not meet the needs of the organization, the L&D department should have the evidence and wit to make a compelling case, and the influence to present it to the relevant part of the leadership team.

It is also possible that when the LMS was purchased, the specification phase of the process fell short. This is utterly possible, as with the major airline that consulted with managers and staff before making a purchasing decision, but after implementation found the LMS was useless for a significant number of its employees. The consultation had only reached the ground staff. Aircrew – perhaps because their roles keep them on the move – had not been consulted. The specification missed out on their particular needs, and the LMS was useless for them. There is lot to be learned from the reaction of the airline, and the way it turned around a difficult situation, as we shall see in Chapter 11.

A more understandable issue is that an LMS – or indeed any learning technology – may be specified and purchased with a particular need in mind, only for the purchasing organization to find after some time that further uses for it become apparent, uses that the system is unable to fulfil. Understandable though this may be, it may also show a lack of proper specification by the L&D department. If buying and implementing an LMS is a significant cost, then getting some sense of likely future usage must be part of the specification process.

There is a further reason why a member of an L&D department might say that the LMS – or any technology – purchased does not meet its needs: too much is expected of it. This may be because the vendor has oversold the product, but the ultimate responsibility rests with the purchaser. In any technology implementation, the first stage is always the 'Discovery' or 'Understanding' phase of analysing the issues at hand. Ultimately, the L&D department must bear the responsibility of running this phase stringently, and ensuring that any technology is capable of the job it was bought for. We are back to the principle underlying Moore's categorization: what is the technology to be used for?

Although I have dealt here with LMSs, the implementation issues they face are those faced by most learning technologies. Initially there must be a clearly spelled-out *aim* – with a well-defined specification to meet an established need. The L&D team must have the right *people* on the implementation team and be able to influence others in the organization effectively. It absolutely must have the wider *perspective* to be able to understand how the organizational environment will change in the future, as well as what new technologies may be available. Finally, the L&D department must take a pragmatic *attitude* to all this – judging for example, where to push a vendor for more functionality, and where a workaround is the best approach.

These four characteristics Aim, People focus, Perspective and Attitude – are the common factors behind those successfully implementing any learning technology. They form the core of Part Two of this book.

Public content platforms

While some L&D departments are struggling to get the most of their LMSs, other content-focused learning platforms have been enthusiastically welcomed into the workplace. Consumer platforms such as Google, YouTube, Wikipedia and iTunes are great sources of free content. Employees frequently use them without considering that they might be learning. And they use them a lot. Google is notoriously secretive on the statistics around its flagship product, but a 2016 estimate of traffic put it at 'single or low double-digits' trillions of searches per year, while YouTube has a billion users (YouTube, 2016). English Wikipedia contains over five million pages of crowdsourced content, voluntarily contributed (Wikipedia, 2016). Any LMS administrator would kill for engagement levels like this.

With the exception of Wikipedia, which is funded by donations and largely run by volunteers, these are consumer products in a uniquely powerful position of being incumbent near-monopolies. They are also extremely profitable and plough a lot of that money back into making their products even more effective. Google's parent company Alphabet Inc. typically spends an eye-watering US $3 billion *per quarter* on research and development (Google, 2016). To be sure, that includes money spent on driverless cars, wearable technologies and so on, but a considerable chunk will have gone towards honing the user experience and functionality of search.

However much the LMS administrator might desire these software giants' functionality, however much the employee might crave their usability, there is simply no comparison between the massive power of consumer-grade public content platforms and the commercial private content platforms usually deployed as learning technologies. This does not stop everyone wanting it. The ubiquity of these powerful engines and their vast array of content have affected users' attitudes considerably, in particular in the following ways:

- Mobile, naturally – Increasingly, users of any system simply expect it to work on a range of smart mobile devices from tablets to smartphones to desktop machines, across browsers and operating systems.

- Training? What training? – Some 10–15 years ago if you introduced a new system into your organization, users would expect training. Increasingly now they expect it to be as intuitive as the stuff they use at home and on their phones, whether it is Netflix, Facebook, iTunes or Twitter.

- User experience by right – These companies have invested hundreds of millions of dollars in their user experience. An experience that is easy and apparently intuitive is the result of corporations relentlessly optimizing algorithms and interfaces until users don't notice, but just expect that experience by right. It is another way consumer brands protect their position as incumbents – by providing the best experience.

- A need for speed – How many items does Amazon have available? Nobody at Amazon will say just how many tens of millions, but you can find what you want almost immediately, and have it delivered to your door within hours. That is the standard users now expect from every online interaction. Today, when an employee wants to know something, they expect the answer immediately, regardless of how much content might need to be searched through.

- Hear me! – Almost every public content platform gives users the opportunity to contribute their view, whether it is to alter a wiki entry or review a product. As article 1 of the Cluetrain Manifesto put it in 1999, 'Markets are conversations'. Contribution is a given and interaction is expected (Cluetrain Manifesto, 1999).

These wonderfully developed platforms set impossibly high standards. There is no way an L&D department can emulate Amazon's back-end processes, Wikipedia's breadth of content, or Google's search algorithms. As it can't, it can instead use these existing, free commercial tools where it can, and emulate – as far as possible – their streamlined user experience by keeping things pared back and as simple as possible. We will explore just how free content fits into the L&D department's overall provision of content in the next chapter.

Wonderful as they are, these public content platforms are imperfect for learning because of the way they are generally used. Employees can waste a tremendous amount of time in search, and the answers they find may be inaccurate or just plain wrong. This is where L&D has a role to play, either in finding and filtering the most commonly searched-for information or in helping employees become smart, digital learners.

And there is one way in which L&D departments can not just match, but can exceed the quality of these huge public platforms of generic content. L&D departments can communicate better with their users, with a greater understanding of the user's context, because they understand the organization and context they're working in. I say only that they *can* do a good job of communication. Most departments generally do not, and especially during a learning technologies implementation, and this probably results in more roll-out failures than any other single factor. We will explore this tricky business of communications in more detail in Chapter 10.

This brief examination of the nature of public and private content platforms is by no means a comprehensive overview of all learning technologies. It is, rather, a way to highlight the tools that learning technologists are most likely to implement (private platforms) and those most likely to inform users' perception of those technologies (public platforms).

Individual learning tools

Our focus on content in this chapter is due to the fact that content technologies dominate the technologies deployed in the workplace. In the 2016–17 Towards Maturity benchmark report, the 10 most widely used learning technologies among the 600 respondent companies were (Towards Maturity, 2016):

1 Live online learning
2 E-learning objects
3 Surveys and questionnaires for understanding
4 Internal platforms (such as SharePoint)
5 Learning Management Systems
6 Communications tools
7 Online assessment for certification
8 Job aids (for example, checklists)
9 Video
10 Mobile devices

Of these, only Communications tools (6) is directly about people sharing information. While Mobile devices (10) may be used for communication, they can also be used to access content, and it is content which dominates the rest of the list, leaving space only for Surveys (3) and Assessment (7).

This corporate overview of learning tools seems to leave little space for Moore's other two categories of interaction – between learners, and between learners and experts. When we look at the private world of learners, however, the view is very different. Since 2000, UK-based Jane Hart has been exploring how people learn at work and the technologies they use to support it. Her C4LPT (Centre for Learning and Performance Technologies) site now receives over 2 million visits annually.

One of the key resources on the site is her annual list of the most popular tools used for learning, compiled from an annual survey that in 2016 saw contributions from 1,238 learning professionals in 64 countries. Originally, this survey produced a single list of the 'Top 100 Tools', but Jane now creates an overall list of 200 tools, and breaks the data down further into three separate lists of 100, for those used in education, personally and at work. Here are the top 10 tools of the list of tools used for personal development (Hart, 2016):

1 Google Search

2 YouTube

3 Twitter

4 Facebook

5 LinkedIn

6 WordPress

7 Skype

8 Wikipedia

9 Google Docs/Drive

10 PowerPoint

In contrast with the Towards Maturity list, here only two items are concerned with content creation: blogging platform WordPress and the presentation software Microsoft PowerPoint. There are twice as many communication tools – Twitter, Facebook, LinkedIn, Skype, and three public content platforms – Google Search, YouTube and Wikipedia.

The personal world of learning technologies, it seems, is very different from the corporate, and much more concerned with communicating and with publicly available information. The only LMS in the top 50 of the full list of 200 tools is Moodle, the open source platform, which ranks 27th. Otherwise, the list is almost devoid of mainstream tools, apart from Microsoft Office applications. Instead of enterprise applications, it is dominated by tools for personal communications, productivity and data storage.

This underlines a shift that Jane has seen in the way people learn. Just as the experience of public content platforms has changed people's expectations of how software should behave, so their experience of the web has, according to Jane, subtly altered how they expect to learn at work. Today, says Jane, people expect learning to be (Hart, 2015):

- Continuous – thanks to the networks they belong to, people are now tapped into a regular stream of information and conversation that accumulates over time into a substantial body of knowledge. This is in contrast to training's packaging of learning into events.

- On demand – when faced with an issue at work (points 3 to 5 of Mosher and Gottfredson's five moments of learning need), people search for an immediate solution, rather than a course and a test. Importantly, they do not expect or need to remember the solution – only where to find it again.

- Concentrated – because most of the issues people face are around immediate performance issues, they tend to want to use short pieces of content with immediate impact, rather than courses.

- Social – people learn not just from, but with others, in communication. The tools to do this are now available commercially and are increasingly expected to be part of working life.

- Embedded – people expect access to these immediate, concentrated opportunities to learn where they are, an expectation reinforced by the wide use of mobile devices.

- Serendipitous – while some learning is planned, much of it is by chance, learning through work and the chance conversations of networks.

- Autonomous – Jane Hart says that this is the key way the web has influenced the way we expect to learn. It gives people control over their access to information and people, for personal and professional development.

This sort of self-directed learning that Jane describes is very different from the traditional experience of centrally driven, prescriptive training. It is worth noting that the data set comes from a group of people who are, by their nature, engaged in learning and enthusiastic enough about it to submit their 10 tools to Jane's list. This self-selecting sample is probably not representative of the working population; the question is whether it is an indicator of where it is heading as a whole. Jane cites research from the Pew Research Internet Project to suggest that it is. Whatever the answer, there is no question that the workforce's approach to learning and technology is changing, bringing with it profound implications for the implementation of learning technologies.

We shall return to the evolving picture of workplace learning and the demands it will likely place on L&D professionals in the final part of this book. As we have seen in this chapter, however, today the L&D function at work is typically focused on the creation and distribution of content, something we explore in more detail in the next chapter.

Key takeaways

1 Trying to categorize learning technologies is a thankless task, but thinking of them using Michael Moore's three types of interactions can be useful.

2 Organizational L&D professionals are most concerned with the interaction between learners and content.

3 Platforms for the private production and distribution of learning content are usually deployed to meet regulatory and administrative demands (for example, of compliance training), rather than to improve the quality of learning.

4 Private content platforms suffer from comparison with public content platforms, which have set high user expectations in terms of functionality, speed and user experience.

5 Research shows that technologies for content production and distribution are by far the most popular category of tools in use within organizations.

6 In contrast, lists of tools that people use personally for learning tend to be dominated by technologies for communication and by public content platforms.

7 This new, personal world of learning is one which we can expect to influence the future use of learning technologies.

References

Cluetrain Manifesto (1999) [accessed 6 December 2016] The Cluetrain Manifesto, [Online] http://cluetrain.com/

Culatta, R (2011) [accessed 26 November 2016] Categorization of Learning Technologies, *Innovative Learning*, [Online] http://innovativelearning.com/instructional_technology/categories.html

Google (2016) [accessed 6 December 2016] Finance Alphabet Inc, [Online] https://www.google.com/finance?q=NASDAQ:GOOG&fstype=ii

Hart, J (2015) [accessed 6 December 2016] Learners are learning differently; are you changing the way you train and support them?, *C4LPT*, 26 March, [Online] http://www.c4lpt.co.uk/blog/2015/03/26/learners-are-learning-differently-are-you-changing-the-way-you-train-them/

Hart, J (2016) [accessed 6 December 2016] Top 200 Tools for Learning 2016: Overview, *C4LPT*, [Online] http://c4lpt.co.uk/top100tools/

Hillman, D, Willis, D and Gunawardena, C (1994) [accessed 26 November 2016] Learner Interface Interaction in Distance Education: An extension of contemporary models and strategies for practitioners, *The American Journal of Distance Education*, 8 (2), pp 30–42, [Online] http://www.tandfonline.com/doi/abs/10.1080/08923649409526853

Medved, J P (2015) [accessed 24 November 2016] LMS Industry User Research Report, *Capterra*, 8 April, [Online] www.capterra.com/learning-management-system-software/user-research

Moore, M (1989) [accessed 26 November 2016] Editorial: Three Types of Interaction, *The American Journal of Distance Education*, 3 (2), pp 1–6, [Online] http://aris.teluq.uquebec.ca/portals/598/t3_moore1989.pdf

Porter, S (2015) [accessed 28 November 2016] I love PowerPoint! *Times Educational Supplement*, 24 November, [Online] https://www.tes.com/news/blog/i-love-powerpoint

Towards Maturity (2016) Unlocking Potential: Releasing the potential of the business and its people through 2016–17 Learning Benchmarking Report, Towards Maturity

Wikipedia (2016) [accessed 6 December 2016] Statistics, [Online] https://en.wikipedia.org/wiki/Wikipedia:Statistics

YouTube (2016) [accessed 6 December 2016] Statistics, [Online] https://www.youtube.com/yt/press/en-GB/statistics.html

Types of content

06

We live in an age of science and of abundance. The care and reverence for books... is no longer suited to... the conservation of learning. EZRA POUND, CHAPTER ONE, *ABC OF READING*, 1934

We have explored what it means for something to be a learning technology and have examined briefly the ways in which learning content can be stored and distributed. In this chapter we go on to explore what exactly we mean by learning content, with particular reference to how we source it. The aim of this chapter is not only to describe, however. It is also to suggest a new relationship between L&D and content very different from the traditional one.

First, I aim to describe a landscape in which content is no longer rare. In the words of the American poet Ezra Pound, we live in an age of abundance. L&D can draw on this abundance, using what already exists, rather than recreating it, and so liberate time for other work. Second, with this, I believe that we will come to abandon the 'care and reverence' for content that Pound speaks of. Increasingly the majority of it will come to be seen as transitory. Third, and finally, L&D's focus on (and sometimes obsession with) controlling content will end. In the past it was our *raison d'être*, in the future it will be just one part of a wider role.

When I began as a classroom trainer in the 1980s, L&D's function was largely to deliver training in the classroom to a regular, often annually published, schedule. This situation continued to the early 21st century. The term 'learning content' was never used. There were courses, and books, and even audio or video cassettes for the more forward-thinking trainers. However, with the spread of e-learning, the breadth and variety of media we could learn from multiplied. With that trend came the term 'e-learning content'; eventually the 'e' fell away as terminology caught up with the fact that we have, for a long time, been living in a world with multiple sources of information.

Today, increasingly, 'learning content' is abbreviated to simply 'content', in realization of the fact that, as natural learners, we can and do learn from anything, whether it was produced with the aim of learning in mind or not. 'Content', then, includes courses and reference materials explicitly produced for learning. It also includes books, magazines, e-books, videos, podcasts and broadcasts, anything, in fact, which can be recorded and distributed in some way. A conference presentation may contain useful information to learn from, but it is not content in this sense. However, the slides from the presentation and the video recording definitely are.

Some learning and development professionals are specialists in producing content for one medium or another – video, say, or e-books – others have a predisposition to using one form over another. As a result, discourse on content tends to focus on the medium and the tools used to produce content for that medium. For this book, though, I will consider content by how it was sourced: where did it come from, and how contextually sensitive is it? This has an important impact on how L&D deals with it, as well as an influence on how it is used with learning technologies.

Thinking about content in this way led me to the 'learning content pyramid' (Taylor, 2013), which drew on a blog by Clive Shepherd (Shepherd, 2008) – itself based on conversations with Nick Shackleton-Jones and others – that suggested three types of content. My 2013 pyramid had five layers, the new version has six. This extra layer includes a recent development where content providers or brokers work with an organization to create 'curated content sets' (Figure 6.1).

The arrow on the left, showing that contextual relevance increases higher up the pyramid, is based on a suggestion by Danish e-learning designer Jakob Gravesen (Gravesen, 2013). The arrow on the right emphasizes the shape of the pyramid, indicating that there is more material available at the bottom than at the top. Usually, although not always, the production values increase as you go further up the pyramid.

From the bottom of the pyramid, the six layers are as follows:

Figure 6.1 The learning content pyramid

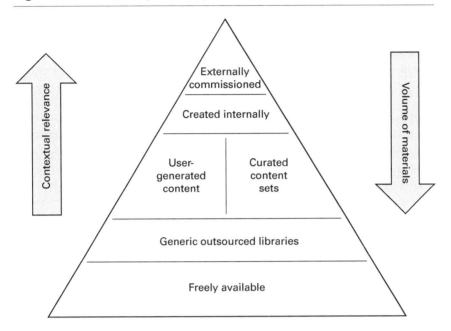

Freely available content

This is content available for free, usually via the internet. For L&D professionals the trick is to build this into organizational learning in a helpful way rather than simply pointing people at a vast array of unfiltered resources. This has been happening for some time. In 2013 in the UK, Virgin Media incorporated content from free language-learning site Duolingo into their corporate LMS (LearningTechUK, 2013). Other organizations do this with free content from iTunes U and YouTube, with TED talks proving especially popular. Massive Open Online Courses (MOOCs) from suppliers such as Coursera, Udemy and FutureLearn also fall into this layer of the pyramid.

Some content available for free on the internet is of very average production value. Some is exceptionally high – as with Duolingo's courses and BBC content. We should not confuse the quality of production with the quality of learning it will support, however. It is possible to create wonderful-looking courses, performance support tools and other assets which, despite their aesthetic appeal, do not help people learn well. And it is quite possible for an unexciting asset to have a tremendous impact on learning and/or performance.

Another assumption to avoid is that free content in the bottom layer of the pyramid is invariably accessed via the internet. In 2013, faced with a 45 per cent budget cut and a reduction of staff from seven to two, Andrew Jacobs turned to whatever free resources he could to support the learning of employees at Lambeth Borough Council. As well as using free online resources, this included pointing staff towards books available via the council's libraries (Gardner, 2013).

Generic content

There is a global market for generic online learning materials. This is content – usually courses – that can be used in a wide variety of situations. A unit on how to create a pie chart in Excel, for example, has a broad application, regardless of what size or type of organization it is used in. Supply of this generic content is dominated by SkillSoft, a global content company headquartered in Dublin, Ireland, which not only owns a considerable, wide-ranging catalogue of material, but also a content delivery platform and an LMS. After merging with SmartForce (see Chapter 2) in 2002, SkillSoft became the most significant global player in this field, valued at US $1.1 billion in 2010 (Bersin, 2010). While the marketplace for content has become more complex since then, there remains demand for this content and before commissioning a course, L&D must always ask who else might have already produced it. Any large organization is likely at some point to have bought libraries of courses on topics such as Microsoft Excel and Word, as well as generic soft-skills courses such as that perennial favourite 'handling a performance review'.

Generic courses will not put the content in the employee's exact context. Sometimes they may not meet the particular standards of production that the L&D or marketing departments would like, but the question to be asked here is simple: do these materials do the job well enough? If they do, then the L&D team's time can be spent on something more strategic than replicating a course.

There is plenty of generic content produced to high production values. Video Arts, (also see Chapter 2) continues to successfully produce high-quality generic management training materials. And while it is impossible by definition for generic courses to relate to specific activities, they can be written for particular sectors. As the generic marketplace for catalogue content matures and is dominated by large players, vendors have developed courses aimed at particular sectors, or one sector in particular. In both Houston, Texas and Aberdeen, Scotland, there are clusters of companies specializing in training only for the oil and gas industry. Before creating a course, it is always worth checking if it already exists.

Curated content sets

There is a lot of material available online, whether free or in catalogues of generic content (which typically run to tens of thousands of courses). So much so, that a time-poor L&D professional can find it difficult to know where to source content and how to organize it for employees. Recognizing this, some providers of generic learning content are now providing what can be called 'curated content sets'. These are collections of content suitable for a particular role, department or territory within an organization. They are more context-specific than content chosen from a catalogue, because they are usually written with a particular job role or sector in mind. A course might, for example, be titled not 'Creating pivot tables in Excel' but 'Pivot tables for sales managers' or 'Pivot tables in supply chain management'.

Although relatively new as an idea, there is potential for this concept to grow. It makes absolute sense for generic content companies to do this, but there is no reason for this service to be confined to them. In the future, we can expect to see niche organizations doing nothing but providing consultation on the best free and generic content available for a particular specialist area of work.

It is also possible for a company to act as a central clearing house for specialist producers of e-learning content. This is the role that OpenSesame has adopted. Founded in 2011, the Portland, Oregon, company provides the complex infrastructure for publishers to upload content and for enterprises to download them. This can be done either piecemeal, or *en masse*, or as part of a curated content set that an OpenSesame consultant has created following an engagement with the enterprise.

User-generated content (UGC)

At work, people naturally create vast amounts of materials which others can learn from, whether it is explicitly designed for learning or not. It could be as generic as the company's annual report, as transitory as a briefing for the next few days, or as rough as some notes from a meeting.

As well as material created inside the organization, user-generated content (UGC) includes material created in online social forums, such as the extensive chat created during the Learning and Skills Group webinars (LSG, 2016) or during Twitter chat meetings.

While the content itself is not paid for, UGC is not entirely free, either. There may be no upfront cost for access to a catalogue, as there is with generic content, but it certainly takes time (and sometimes money) to set up and maintain the systems for sharing UGC. And there is more than technology involved here – simply collecting content in one place is not enough. Content that is useful in theory is useless in practice if it cannot be found. To allow it to be found, it needs at the very least a good filing system or search mechanism. It may also need interpretation to put the content in context. Also, it is usual for the value of some UGC to decay over time, and at some point it may need to be removed from the collection. The L&D jargon for looking after other people's content is *curation*. The alternative to curation is too often that a collection of UGC becomes bloated and unwieldy and loses its credibility.

Internally created UGC meets the needs of the organization in a way that generic content never can, because it is written in context. The challenge for much UGC is that the context can be too specific. If the author works in marketing, the content might not necessarily apply in finance or operations. If this is the case, then the L&D

department may wish to intervene to edit or otherwise augment the content.

Another concern with UGC lies with its accuracy. An L&D department steeped in the tradition of providing all courses used by an organization will find it difficult to let go of the reins and allow the free flow of information between employees. This is a fair point – after all, repairing the damage done by putting bad practice into circulation is far more time consuming than preventing it getting into circulation it the first place. On the other hand, organizations need rapid distribution of information to meet the demands of the modern working world.

The solution is for the L&D department to take a pragmatic approach to balancing the need for speed against the risk of bad practice. How bad is the risk, and how likely is it? Sometimes, 'good enough' information that reaches the point of need fast is far better than perfectly accurate information that arrives too late to be of any use. If the severity and likelihood of risk are both low, then L&D can step aside.

On other occasions, there is a need to balance speed with accuracy. When Black & Decker (now Stanley Black & Decker) gave their sales force Flip cameras to record videos for colleagues to view, the videos were not immediately posted onto the Black & Decker platform. They went to the central L&D team, which first checked and tagged before posting them (Albright *et al*, 2011).

And sometimes, only 100 per cent accuracy will do. If there is a risk of a severely dangerous outcome, then even if that risk is very low, the L&D function has a duty to ensure that material is thoroughly and expertly vetted before it is disseminated.

Content created internally

Whereas L&D departments were once the main providers of learning content, now internally created materials have to compete with a vast amount of free or low-cost content and UGC. To justify the necessary commitment of resources, any content created internally must relate to the organization in ways that other forms of content cannot.

While it can be beautifully prepared or emotionally engaging, internally generated content need not be. It need only be context-rich, steeped in the reality of the organization, and useful. It may also be that the content is confidential and unique to the organization, in which case L&D certainly should be involved in managing the content distribution.

When power tool manufacturer TTI wanted to improve efficiency in handling returned goods, it produced a clear, online course covering the 10 most common mistakes in handling returned goods. It was not complex to produce. It did, however, generate US $35 million in savings for the company over a two-year period (Infor, 2012). We will learn more about this case study in Chapter 9.

The key for such content is that it should be contextually rich and valuable. The longer a piece of content is likely to be in use, and the more it is seen as representing the values of the organization, the higher the production values it needs. For highly important materials, L&D will typically turn to outside providers for help, and commission the content.

Commissioned content

Organizations cannot always produce what they need, which is why there will always be a place for high-quality commissioned content. The subject may require specialist knowledge. The high-profile nature of the work may demand great production values, or specialist techniques. Those specialist techniques may, however, only have a short shelf life, and if there is no rush for the content, it is always worth waiting for the skills to become more widely spread. When the use of smartphones for accessing content took off in 2013–14 there was a boom in demand for the services of specialist companies capable of producing suitable content for smartphones. In particular, there was a demand for content that could adapt to different devices, and companies were prepared to pay for the expertise to deliver that. Already, at the time of writing (late 2016) those skills are becoming more commonplace both across a wider range of vendors and within L&D departments' own design teams.

This pyramid is only one way of considering the content that organizations use for learning, but it is a tool that I have found useful to help people think about their own approach to learning content. It tends to prompt questions such as:

- Are we spending too much time creating our own content?
- How high do our production values have to be for this content?
- Are we using our internal (non L&D) experts well enough?
- What free resources could we benefit from?
- What is our most important content, and how should it look?
- What sort of content do we need to support this particular task?

It is worth bearing in mind that the shape of the pyramid is a fiction. It the pyramid were drawn to scale, with each layer reflecting the amount of material available, it would not be a pyramid at all. Rather, it would resemble an enormous pancake, perhaps the size of one of the Great Lakes with an insignificant bump in the middle the size of an upturned soup plate. That vast pancake would be the lowest layer – the super-abundant 'freely available' layer of the internet. The soup plate would be the UGC. On top of the soup plate would be a thimble, representing content created or outsourced. The pancake is huge and growing faster than the rest of the pyramid, and this super-abundance of free material is the miracle of the information age, one we regularly ignore, possibly because it is almost incomprehensible.

With so much information available for free, and with vast amounts of UGC created in large organizations, L&D cannot continue to operate on the model that worked when I began as a trainer in the 1980s – focused on creating and delivering courses. Not only is the task impossible for today's fast-moving workplace, it is an ineffective way of building skills and knowledge, and attempting it absorbs the time that L&D could use for other, more effective activity. It is time to move to a different set of skills, a skillset we will examine in more detail in Part Three. This skillset includes a shift from creating content to curating it. It also includes widening L&D's focus to encompass the creation of learning experiences and developing individuals' ability to learn. All this involves adopting new ways of working, something we explore in detail in the next chapter as we consider a range of models of change.

Key takeaways

1 Learning content (or just 'content') has long been a primary concern of organizational L&D. In the past this has meant creating almost all of it. Today there is considerable opportunity for using content from elsewhere.

2 The internet provides a vast repository of freely available materials to learn from.

3 Some vendors have specialized in creating considerable online libraries of generic content, a useful way of training for some tasks.

4 To help organizations find the right content for particular roles, some companies now offer a consulting service to create curated content sets that effectively package sets of third-party content.

5 A great amount of valuable content is created at work that has the benefit of being highly relevant to the context of the organization. Making the most of this UGC is one of the great opportunities and challenges faced by L&D departments today.

6 Creating original content was once the main role of the L&D department. This is such a time-consuming activity that it should only be undertaken when there is no viable alternative. Good reasons for creating content internally include where content is urgent, relates to high-risk issues and/or is confidential.

7 Some content is so important that it is worth commissioning from specialist production houses. This includes in particular 'flagship' content that expresses the values of the organization, or which is likely to have a long shelf life.

8 Although currently focused on the creation or sourcing of content, and on its delivery, in the future, L&D's role is likely to widen considerably.

References

Albright, S, Bailey, M and Walker, D (2011) [accessed 25 November 2016] Next Learning Unwrapped, *Learn-on-the-Go-Podcasts, Videocasts, and Mobile Learning*, Chapter 5, pp 27–31, [Online] https://issuu.com/ elearningevent/docs/chapter_5_next_learning

Bersin, J (2010) [accessed 8 December 2016] SkillSoft goes private – acquired by private equity, February 2010, [Online] http://cedma-europe.org/ newsletter%20articles/Brandon%20Hall/SkillSoft%20goes% 20private%20-%20acquired%20by%20private%20equity%20 (Feb%2010).pdf

Gardner, I (2013) [accessed 8 December 2016] LearningPool Live South, *Whose education is it anyway?*, 28 October, [Online] https:// whoseeducationisitanyway.me/2013/10/28/learningpool-live-south/

Gravesen, J (2013) [accessed 8 December 2016] Model til inddeling af læringsindhold, *E-læring & Træning*, 15 March, [Online] http:// cadpeople.blogspot.co.uk/2013/03/model-til-inddeling-af-lringsindhold. html

Infor (2012) [accessed 8 December 2016] Techtronic Industries enhances revenue and profitability with Infor Learning Management, [Online] http://www.infor.com/company/registration/?requestedContent= %2Fcontent%2Fcasestudies%2Ftechtronic-industries-company. pdf%2F&ok=yes

LearningTechUK (2013) [accessed 8 December 2016] LSG Webinar: Drop the e, the social, the virtual – it's just learning, Mike Leavy, *Virgin Media*, watch at 41:30, [Online] from https://www.youtube.com/ watch?v=CXmNufU6APw

LSG (2016) [accessed 8 December 2016] Learning and Skills Group webinar archive, [Online] http://learningandskillsgroup.ning.com/ forum/categories/lsg-webinars/listForCategory

Shepherd, C (2008) [accessed 8 December 2016] Three Tiers in the Content Pyramid, *Clive on learning*, 4 June, [Online] http://clive-shepherd.blogspot.co.uk/2008/06/three-tiers-in-content-pyramid. html#!/2008/06/three-tiers-in-content-pyramid.html

Taylor, D (2013) [accessed 8 December 2016] The Learning Content Pyramid, *Donald H Taylor*, 12 March, [Online] https://donaldhtaylor. wordpress.com/2013/03/12/the-learning-content-pyramid/

PART TWO
Implementing learning technologies

Change, models and process 07

... there is nothing more difficult to take in hand, more perilous to conduct, or more uncertain in its success, than to take the lead in the introduction of a new order of things. NICCOLÒ MACHIAVELLI, *THE PRINCE*

When he wrote those words at the beginning of the 16th century, Niccolò Machiavelli was drawing on a lifetime of experience in the turbulent world of Renaissance Italy's warring princedoms. He knew how difficult change was, and that the root of this difficulty lay not in technology (barely even a consideration then) but in people: their beliefs, expectations and preconceptions. He also knew very well that the penalty for introducing change badly was too often a drawn-out, painful death.

When implementing learning technology today, our lives may not be at risk as they were in Machiavelli's time but besides that little has changed. Change can still be difficult, and the reason is simple. In looking at the successes, partial successes and glaring failures of learning technology implementations that I have come across over the past 16 years, it is clear that any challenges in implementing technology come down to the people involved. Andy Wooler, veteran of many Learning Management Systems (LMS) implementations, and currently Academy Technology Manager at Hitachi Data Systems puts it succinctly: 'You can do anything with technology, but people can also stop you doing just about everything.'

This observation of Andy's sums up what is needed to succeed in implementing any learning technology. The technical implementation must follow the right process to go smoothly. However, any implementation also involves people who may derail it at any point. A successful implementation team, I have observed, deals with this risk by demonstrating a set of four characteristics, as well as by following a clear process. Both these factors – the team characteristics and the process – are essential to success. We deal with the four team characteristics in succeeding chapters. This chapter is dedicated to the process that I believe observation shows is common to successful implementations.

Reflecting on a range of organizations' actions in successful learning technology implementations, I believe they can be described in six stages that fall in complexity somewhere between grand models of organizational transformation and the sequential steps used to run a well-organized project. We will look at these models shortly. First, there is a question worth asking: do we really need another model?

Do we really need another model?

There are plenty of models already in the fields of L&D, project management and change management. Is there really any need for another? In compiling my research for this book I fought against it. First, I looked across all the case studies I was examining and boiled their success down to a checklist, along the lines suggested by Atul Gawande's marvellous *The Checklist Manifesto* (Gawande, 2011).

When my checklist reached 17 items, I realized (perhaps a little late) that it was not possible to provide a single prescriptive checklist for all learning technology implementations. Clearly the situation called for something at a higher level – a model. Not wanting to reinvent the wheel, I turned to existing models of change/project management and of technology implementation.

Each of these many models has something to offer. I was hopeful that one would adequately describe the unique factors of a learning technology implementation, including the need to overcome the schoolroom assumption and the necessity of combining sometimes quite intricate project management with the equally complex, but entirely different, need to understand the real drivers to, and objections against, the implementation.

It may not be a surprise that in the end I was unable to find a model that fitted the range of case studies I was familiar with. To give the background to this, and to explain why I thought it necessary to introduce yet another model into the field of L&D, let's examine a few of the key models out there.

Existing models of implementation and change

What follows is an examination of just a handful of the many excellent models of implementation and change in circulation. If you are implementing a learning technology at any sort of scale, it is worth making yourself familiar with these models. They are the result of a great deal of thinking and practical experience.

Kotter's 8-step model

You can't talk about organizational change without talking about John P Kotter. His 1996 book *Leading Change* (Kotter, 1996) set the tone for a swathe of change management books that followed. The 8-step model looks like this, as described by his consultancy (Kotter International, 2014):

Step 1 – Create a sense of urgency

Step 2 – Build a guiding coalition

Step 3 – Form a strategic vision and

Step 4 – Enlist a volunteer army

Step 5 – Enable action by removing barriers

Step 6 – Generate short-term wins

Step 7 – Sustain acceleration

Step 8 – Institute change

In 2014, alongside the original model, Kotter International (the consultancy spawned by his research) introduced the Accelerate 8-Step Process. Whereas the 1996 process is linear and typically driven by a small, focused group, in the Accelerate process, all 8 steps take place concurrently and continuously, and are led by 'a large volunteer army from up, down and across the organization'.

There is a great deal that anyone implementing learning technologies can take from Kotter's model, especially the emphasis on getting people on board and the importance of generating and celebrating short-term wins (Step 6). The final point, too – *Institute change*, that is, embed it in the organization – is essential, but too often overlooked.

Kotter's model, though, is meant for fundamental, transformative changes, the sort that require a company-wide vision to be articulated and bought into. A learning technology may be part of such a transformation, but it will never be the whole of it. While it is certainly a point of reference, this cannot be a model for the detail of implementing learning technologies.

Lewin's Unfreeze-Change-Freeze model

Even more fundamental than Kotter's model is that of Kurt Lewin. Lewin explained organizational change through the metaphor of a block of ice, giving his approach the catchy moniker of the 'Unfreeze-Change-Freeze' model. Imagine you have a volume of water frozen in the form of a cube, but you want it to be in the shape of a cone. You will have to unfreeze the cube, change it into the new shape (presumably by pouring it into a mould) and then freeze it again.

Organizational change, of course, is not quite as simple, and people are not as fluid as water. Like Kotter, Lewin focuses on the difficulties people have with the issues of change. He notes that the Unfreeze part of the process is particularly difficult as individuals need both a compelling reason to change *from* the current state (often they must be forced to confront something they have been satisfied with for years) and be given the motivation to change *towards* the desired state, which is often difficult to visualize and may be uncomfortable for some people. Once a change has been made there is no guarantee that it will stick. In fact, it is likely, observes Lewin, that it will not (Lewin, 1947):

> A change towards a higher level of group performance is frequently short-lived, after a 'shot in the arm', group life soon returns to the previous level. This indicates that it does not suffice to define the objective of planned change in group performance as the reaching of a different

level. Permanency of the new level, or permanency for a desired period, should be included in the objective.

There are similarities here with Kotter's model, particularly in the emphasis on the need to create a compelling picture of a future destination. In implementing learning technologies this still has to be done – not perhaps at the level of a grand, overarching vision or new set of values, but by focusing instead on more practical issues such as a clear articulation of benefits, of the positive impact on existing procedures.

Shewhart/Deming Plan-Do-Check-Act cycle

While Kotter and Lewin and others describe the big picture of organizational change well, the celebrated PDCA model (Plan-Do-Check-Act) model of W Edwards Deming (based on original work by Walter Shewhart) is explicitly a model of process improvement. Here, the aim is not to transform the organization, but to make some of its constituent parts work better.

Just as Kotter is synonymous with organizational change, so Deming and the PDCA cycle are synonymous with process improvement, and for good reasons. The American Deming is revered in Japan where he worked in the 1950s and where he is widely credited with playing a leading role in the country's post-war economic boom, thanks to methods for high-quality design and production. For his catalytic role in Japan's economic renaissance, Deming was awarded the Order of the Sacred Treasure, Second Class in 1960.

The original PDCA cycle was – according to Imai – a recasting of what Deming had presented in a key seminar in 1950 on statistical quality control for managers and engineers (Imai, 1986):

1 Design the product.

2 Make and test it.

3 Market it.

4 Test the market response.

5 Redesign the product (ie restart the cycle).

Deming was explicit that this cyclical, non-linear process was a direct descendent of the work of his colleague Walter Shewhart, who in 1939 suggested that while production was traditionally considered a linear process – from specification to production to inspection – these three steps would be better considered in a cycle, with the result of inspection feedback into changes in the specification (Shewhart and Deming, 1987).

There are several things we can take from the work of Deming and Shewhart, but one stands out. The creation of anything that will be used (in Deming/Shewhart's case a product for a market, in our case a technology for an organization) is most successful when it is developed iteratively. Nobody ever has all the answers at the outset. Only by working with those that need the product/technology can it be honed to the right shape for their use. Shewhart expressed this idea in terms of the scientific method (Shewhart and Deming, 1987):

> These three steps must go in a circle instead of in a straight line, as shown... It may be helpful to think of the three steps in the mass production process as steps in the scientific method. In this sense, speci-fication, production, and inspection correspond respectively to making a hypothesis, carrying out an experiment, and testing the hypothesis. The three steps constitute a dynamic scientific process of acquiring knowledge.

In other words, for Shewhart, as for Deming, the change process is not a matter of imposition, but a way of progressively finding what works – it is a *dynamic process*. It may come as a shock to contemporary, hipster software engineers that the minimum viable product (MVP) is no modern invention, but a pre-Second World War concept dreamed up by statisticians who usually went to work in suits and ties.

It is worth noting that in adopting this approach, the Japanese were unrelenting in the Check part of the cycle. This is expressed very well by Kaoru Ishikawa in his exploration of quality control: 'If standards and regulations are not revised in six months, it is proof that no one is seriously using them' (Ishikawa, 1985).

Few change methods have been as well tested as this approach of Shewhart and Deming, which was not only used by the Japanese in the 1950s, but again by the Americans in the 1980s when the world's largest economic power stood amazed at the progress of the second and sought to emulate it by introducing many ideas created or stimulated by Deming, such as total quality control.

The Shewhart/Deming approach is excellent in its stress on cyclical adaptation. Just as an iterative approach enables a product to be fine-tuned to a market, so it can help a learning technology bed in effectively within an organization. And this iterative approach must survive beyond the launch of the technology. Continued success depends on continuous checking and adaptation well after the technology is in use.

Valuable though it is, the PDCA approach is incomplete for learning technologies, which require considerable work before the iterative process of improving the technology can begin. This need to understand the nature of any proposed change, and how it involves and affects the people and processes of the organization is something dealt with better when we consider models for implementing technologies in general.

Technology implementation models

While the Shewhart/Deming approach focuses on process, technology implementation models include more of the human element, which experience shows is consistently where technology succeeds or fails. One of these models is that of Melanie Franklin, who proposes a deceptively simple four-stage process (Franklin, 2011):

1 Understand the change.

2 Plan and prepare for the change.

3 Implement the change.

4 Embed the change.

The devil, as always, is in the detail. Franklin suggests a number of tools for understanding the issues, as well as for planning and preparing for change, but as with every good model, she makes it clear that the human element is key. In the 'Understand' phase, for example, she stresses the importance of answering the question 'What's in it for me?' for everyone touched by a technology implementation. This extends from the upper echelons of an organization to those touched directly by use of the technology.

And after implementation, Franklin stresses the crucial issue of people slipping back post-transition: 'The desire to return to the old ways should never be underestimated.' She gives two instances of when this is likely – when a new way of working does not take into account special, one-off transactions that the old process recognized, and in times of pressure, when people naturally slip into old habits.

While these are clearly issues for – for example – large enterprise-wide software implementations, they might seem less pressing for learning technologies, which are not as wide-ranging in scope. However, when it comes to the fundamental change of altering how a person learns something, or finds out information, preventing post-transition regression is an absolute necessity. The classic instance is when an e-learning system is introduced, only to be ignored, while employees continue to demand classroom training. Why? Almost certainly because nobody properly addressed the desires and working habits of the people involved, involving them in the process, rather than treating them as objects to be manipulated by it.

The Association for Project Management

From Kotter, Lewin, Deming/Shewhart and Franklin it is clear that successfully introducing any major change (including a technology-focused one) involves understanding the impact it will have on people, iterating during implementation, and continuing to check the state of both the technology and the people it affects.

What makes for success during implementation of the technology? In 2014 The Association for Project Management (APM), based in the UK, published *Factors in Project Success* (APM, 2014) in conjunction with BMG Research, which gathered input from more than 800 project managers, split equally between APM members and non-members. Respondents were asked to give their feedback on the APM's framework of 12 factors contributing to project success.

Perhaps unsurprisingly, the report found that no single factor will ensure project success on its own, but of the factors identified (including those suggested by respondents), three stood out as important to project success. In declining order of their presence on typical projects, they are:

1 Capable project teams

2 Effective governance

3 Goals and objectives

In this case, effective governance means having 'clear structures and responsibilities for decision-making in place, with clear reporting lines between individuals and groups involved in project management and delivery'. The three factors could be summarized as 'knowing what you have to do, knowing who has to do what, and being able to do it'.

Vendor methodologies

At the other end of the scale from the big picture, change management models are the very specific implementation methodologies used by software vendors. You cannot implement a significant platform without one, and any vendor of any quality will have a methodology that has been written on the back of hard-learned lessons in the field. Because they are so practical, and based on real experiences, they are definitely worth examining. When choosing a vendor, make the methodology a part of your selection process. If they don't have one, or it looks flimsy, it is worth asking them why.

A challenge to the idea of change management

Anyone who has worked in an organization of any size will be familiar with the idea of centrally driven projects. They will also be familiar with the reactions they frequently invoke: helplessness, hostility and indifference being more common than avid enthusiasm.

One of the most articulate voices suggesting that management needs to severely question our addiction to such programmes is management iconoclast and Visiting Professor of Strategic and International Management at London Business School, Gary Hamel. In 2014, Hamel suggested in a compelling 2014 editorial for consulting firm McKinsey that companies should 'Build a change platform, not a change program' (Hamel and Zanini, 2014). In this critique, Hamel says there are three interconnected strands that cripple change management programmes.

First, change management programmes start at the top of the organization, and by the time they are big enough to be perceived as important by the top of the organization it is already too late. Companies are, in Hamel's words 'playing defense', and combined with the risk-aversion of some management, the result is that change management programmes are usually too little, too late.

Second, change is rolled out. The result – employees feel this is something that is being done *to* them, which they simply have to put up with. The emphasis of models such as Kotter's and Lewin's on buy-in is a necessity, according to this critique, because the change is being imposed on people. Instead, suggests Hamel, the change effort should be 'socially constructed... people aren't against change – they are against royal edicts'.

Finally, he says, change is 'engineered'. In other words, it tends to be driven from the top to a plan, as if changing an organization were no more complex than assembling a piece of flat-pack furniture according to the instructions. The reality, he says, is that change – especially if it is fundamental – is impossible to plan and implement step-by-step, and taking such a top-down approach inevitably means that those writing the plan miss the breadth of experience and input which the implementers – those involved in the organization's work day-to-day – could bring.

Hamel suggests an alternative to top-down notions of change, giving three shifts in approach:

- From top-down to activist-out
- From sold to invited
- From managed to organic

This sort of 'socially-constructed change' is not easy to manage, and it is neither quick nor easy, but, he points out, it is possible and it is effective.

I have focused on Gary Hamel's ideas here because they are always worth listening to and because great work has been done using his approach of socially constructed change. This method is clearly sound in some instances. In some very large, very disparate organizations such as the UK's National Health Service, it may be the only way to build fundamental transformations of behaviour. Whether this approach can also be used to implement information technology that needs to work with other enterprise-wide systems is debatable, but the key point here is Hamel's focus on the source of the driving force in change. Change pushed from the top is likely to be at best slow and partial. Change that represents in some way the collective will of those in an organization, and which works for them, is likely to be faster, and capable of being sustained through difficult times.

How is learning technology different?

Just how is learning technology different from other technologies? And if it is not different, why does it need its own implementation methodology?

Technically, learning technologies are no different from any other enterprise-wide system. Each requires people to do things with an information technology system, usually at a computer or computer-like device, and data around this activity is collected and tracked. From this point of view, a Learning Management System is little different from, for example, an Enterprise Resource Planning (ERP) system for managing a manufacturing process or a Customer Relationship Management (CRM) system for tracking sales activity.

While there may be little technical difference in the software involved, there are absolutely fundamental differences between ERP/CRM systems and learning technologies as far as the wetware is concerned (wetware being the slightly revolting term software engineers occasionally use for people).

The two key differences are the preconceptions of the people using the technology, and the impact that technology is supposed to have.

We examined the key preconception facing any learning technology in Part One – the schoolroom assumption, the idea that learning is somehow equivalent to training, which is best done sitting down, listening to an expert in a physical classroom. As discussed, this preconception runs deep across management, employees and frequently in the Learning and Development department, too. It is this preconception that has led to the bizarre idea that people will somehow learn efficiently if information is parcelled up and delivered to them.

No other enterprise-wide information technology implementation has to deal with such deeply entrenched preconceptions. This affects the entire implementation, from initial conversations with executives and managers to understanding how employees choose to learn and the best ways of supporting their performance. It means that any learning technology implementation must go beyond the project management approach of, for example, the APM and Melanie Franklin, and include some of the cultural change aspects in the classic change management models of Kotter and Lewin. A learning technology implementation is never only about the technology. It always challenges this deeply embedded assumption.

The other way in which learning technologies are not just another information technology is in what they do and don't do. They help people learn. In doing so, they change the way people work, to the benefit of the organization, but usually intangibly and often over a period of time.

This is fundamentally different from other systems. An organizational implementation of an ERP system may, for instance, help employees deal with customers more effectively, or perhaps give them more control over the supply chain. Almost always the system is enabling an existing process, and its positive impact is apparent. Perhaps customer calls are logged better, or inventory stock is reduced. In contrast, the impact of learning is almost always invisible (there will be an impact, but an explicit effort must be made to quantify it). The result is that managers have to be persuaded to allow time for employees to use the technology, when that time could often be spent doing something with more immediately evident impact on this week's targets. Again, this means that implementing a learning technology is never a mere technical challenge. There is a huge role to play in winning over managers – the people in any organization who decide how time is spent.

But while learning technologies do change people's behaviour through learning, this does not mean their implementations are substantial change programmes. These sorts of programmes – the sort that Hamel so eloquently rails against – are characterized by a major shift in values or attitudes, something that does not happen with a learning technology implementation beyond a challenge to the schoolroom assumption. These big change programmes are more ambitious than implementing a learning technology. They are also – almost certainly because of that ambition – less likely to succeed. Kotter reckons 70 per cent of them fail.

Learning technology implementations, then, fall somewhere between the grand change programmes aiming to shift the values of an organization and a regular enterprise technology implementation, and on balance are typically more like the latter than the former.

A process model for learning technology implementations

I hope that I have made it clear that I believe there is a case for a separate process model for learning technologies implementations that is not as substantial as the organizational change models of Kotter and Lewin, but which goes beyond the focus on implementation of the APM's study and Franklin's model, for example.

None of these models is wrong, of course. Each persists because it has been found valuable, echoing statistician George Box's famous dictum that 'All models are wrong, but some are useful'. And for any one implementing learning technologies, each does have something salient to offer: Kotter and Lewin's focus on people and motivation as determining the success of any change; Deming/Shewhart's focus on relentless testing and the insistence that production be a cycle, rather than a linear process. The APM's research shows the importance of forming the right project teams under good governance and, with Franklin, insists on proper project planning for the implementation phase.

In considering existing good work in this field (including, but not limited to, the models mentioned here), and in discussion with many others, I concluded that it is possible to create a process model which both captures the uniqueness of L&D and combines it with the good sense of other models.

This attempt to model the process of learning technology implementation echoes the other models referenced in this chapter, including their emphasis on iteration and on discovery, as well as including that elusive quality of successful learning technology implementations: that they always combine a shared clarity of purpose with a pragmatic approach to achieving it.

The six steps in this proposed process are:

1 Understand the issues at stake, the people involved.

2 Plan the implementation.

3 Test the plan, usually with a pilot.

4 Implement the technology.

5 Assess the impact.

6 Sustain the implementation.

Too often, learning technology implementations fail because they start with Planning, rather than Understanding, then jump to Implementation skipping over the need to Test first. By leaping straight into the intricacies of the implementation itself, and ignoring the need for scoping, the L&D team fails to understand the precise business needs, and the people who may support or impede the implementation.

If starting too fast is one issue that typically trips up learning technology implementations, the other is finishing too soon. Too often an implementation team puts a system of some sort in place without also putting in place anything to ensure its long-term maintenance. This is a recipe for eventual failure. No technology will run for ever unmaintained, which is one reason the final stage is so important.

The six steps are shown diagrammatically in Figure 7.1.

Figure 7.1 The six-step model

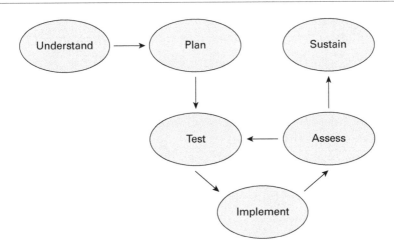

Waterfall or agile?

As Figure 7.1 shows, the middle three stages – Test, Implement and Assess – may occur once, in sequence. Alternatively, they may occur more than once, iteratively, echoing Shewhart and Deming's PDCA cycle. When they are carried out just once, this is the traditional waterfall approach to roll out, usually associated with a single, 'big-bang' launch of the technology during the implementation phase.

The second, sequential, approach is more agile, where the L&D team cycles through the three stages iteratively, improving the implementation each time in response to the assessment, testing the changes, implementing them, and then altering them again, with each iteration bringing the implementation closer to optimal. (For more on the agile approach to software development, see Chapter 12.)

Once this idea of a product or service staying in beta (that is, not reaching its final stage of production) for an extended period would have been frowned on. However, agile software development and some prominent examples have made the idea of 'perpetual beta' unremarkable today. Google Mail was in beta for five years before finally having the 'beta' label removed.

Understand

The Understand step is fundamental – it sets the direction for the rest of the implementation and provides guidance around likely allies and partners as well as potential barriers. Consultants sometimes label this phase 'Discovery', in the sense that the consultants should not come into an organization with preconceptions, but should rather uncover what is already there.

Before considering what happens during this step, let's consider some different possible routes into using learning technologies. The most important question – because it affects the likely level of initial support – is where the idea came from to begin with. Whose idea was it? It could have come from the L&D department, from someone at an operational level in the organization, or it could be a directive from the organization's leadership. These will all affect the approach that the L&D department can take.

Another key consideration is whether the technology has already been bought or not. Ideally, the decision to buy software would only come after a clearly structured consideration of a business need and a proper procurement process. Ideally. In reality, there may already be a technology solution in place for a number of reasons. It may be that the organization has invested in a substantial Enterprise Resource Planning platform such as Oracle, SAP or Infor. In such cases it is usual for the finance or IT departments to require the use of the learning technologies integrated into these packages. It may be that the L&D department bought the technology some time ago, and is now seeking to implement it to tackle a particular need. It may even be that there is no need to actually purchase software, because it is free, or because – as with LinkedIn, Facebook, WordPress and other tools – it is a widely available consumer product already used by some employees.

Whoever came up with the idea of using learning technology, whether it is already in place or not, three questions will need to be answered during the Understand step.

What is the business issue?

There must be a sound business reason for the implementation. Without this, there is no chance of the implementation succeeding in the long term, and no reason why it should. By contrast, a clear business issue makes it possible to state clearly what a successful implementation will look like.

What is the political landscape?

The expression of a clear business issue does not guarantee the enthusiastic support of key stakeholders in the organization. A key part of the understanding step is to learn the political landscape surrounding the implementation, as well as the legitimate hurdles to the implementation at different levels of the organization – particularly in terms of the possible impact on existing ways of working.

What is the technical position?

Technical issues are cast in the light of the identified business issue and the political landscape surrounding them. Every technical issue can be solved with resources or compromise, but only by having a business issue worth tackling can the political will be summoned to provide either.

The Understand step is explored in detail in Chapter 9.

Plan

Tackling these three key questions in the Understand step does not quite leave you free to begin planning immediately. First, it is necessary to be sure you have all your resources available – including in particular your team.

Assembling the team

Most L&D departments are focused on particular skills such as content production and delivery, not on project management, marketing or IT implementation. A crucial initial step at the beginning of the planning phase is to identify what skills and knowledge an implementation will need, what exists in the department, and – before the rest of the planning takes place – building the right team for the job.

Creating a plan without contributions from an experienced team is a great way to build a plan that won't work.

It is also crucial to consider the other people necessary to the plan's success, the non-core team. These could include a governance board and vendor representatives who can't be on the main implementation team. We explore the people side of an implementation in more detail in Chapter 10, and understanding where a team's skills need bolstering in Chapter 12.

Plan the technical implementation

With the team in place, it should be possible to plan the technical implementation. The complexity of this will range from negligible (for a departmental use of microblogging tool Yammer, for example) to large (for, say, an enterprise-wide implementation of a learning management system). Once a plan is written, there is a temptation to regard it as cast in stone. One role of the non-core, advisory team is to keep challenging it during implementation, and changing it where necessary, while remaining on target to achieve the overall aim. Providing input and feedback to the team around the plan is also one important role of communications.

Plan communications

Communications is too often seen as a 'push' exercise, with the sole object of convincing previously unaware employees of the benefits of a particular learning programme. Good communications are very far from that. They are a true dialogue that involve listening as much as telling and play a vital part in adapting and optimizing the implementation.

Test

Testing is where the plan meets reality, and where that reality bites. For the testing process to be of any use, the feedback it provides has to be captured and used to improve the implementation. This applies both to testing technical issues and user experience.

Build the test process

Ensure you have a structured testing process, and ways of capturing anomalies and feeding them into a process for fixing them. Ensure also that the testing process is adequately staffed with people who know what they are doing.

Technical testing

Test functionality. Does the technology work as expected? Is it compliant with internal and external requirements (for example, the international W3C standards on accessibility)? It is obviously crucial to test the technical requirements – for example, bandwidth and hardware requirements – across the organization, being sure to include areas where the technical infrastructure is weakest.

Testing process impact

Some learning technologies will have no impact on business processes. Others can have a considerable impact. The worst thing that can happen to any workplace technology implementation is when afterwards someone says 'Oh yeah, the system says A, but we always do B'. When workarounds and shortcuts increase following a technology implementation, that implementation has failed. In Chapter 8 we explore the detailed analysis The Hershey Company made of its processes when implementing an LMS.

Testing usability, reaction and impact

The implementation may work technically and may have a benign impact on processes, but if it doesn't meet the defined business goal, it is pointless. The testing phase has to include assessment of reaction to the implementation from all stakeholders, but particularly from those who will be using it most intensively, with a particular focus on testing usability. In addition there must be some assessment of how effectively the original business goal is being targeted. The Herman Miller case study in Chapter 10 explores one good method of gathering feedback by using online focus groups.

Implement

For organizations adopting an agile approach, the implementation phase will be stepped through many times (as will the phases of piloting and testing) until the final implementation is deemed to meet the needs of the organization. In contrast, an organization adopting a waterfall approach will only implement once, with minor adjustments to the implementation perhaps taking place in the next step of assessment.

At least, that's what the theory says. In practice, the three clearly delineated steps of the implementation phase: Test, Implement and Assess overlap in most learning technology implementations. In particular, some assessment will always take place concurrently with the other two steps, and with it the need to adjust and alter the implementation immediately, when necessary. The best-laid plans usually fail to survive contact with reality. If the implementation step is regarded as the step where a predetermined plan is followed through, then it is likely to fail. Here, above all, flexibility in method – combined with relentless focus on the end goal – is essential.

Implementing the communications plan

Communications will lead any technical implementation – setting expectations, building buy-in and establishing feedback mechanisms. To an extent the communications part of the implementation step is only a more formally fleshed-out version of the communication and stakeholder engagement that has already been taking place, and which continues long after implementation, during the Assess and Sustain steps. For an example of combining stakeholder analysis with communications plans, see Chapter 10.

Implementing the technology plan

The complexity of the learning technology implementation itself will vary according to the technology involved, but will certainly involve the following considerations:

- **Integration** – to what extent is the learning technology integrated with other systems, in particular with the organizational Human Resources Information Systems (HRIS)?

- **Configuration/customization** – how far is the learning technology adapted to the particular circumstances of the organization, and what are the implications for ongoing maintenance?

- **Migration** – in many cases the particular technology may be the second or third attempt to get a particular platform right. This is particularly true for LMS implementations. Is data migration from legacy systems part of the implementation, and if so, what will be migrated and what left behind?

Go live

As discussed at the start of this chapter, there are different ways to launch an implementation. Some organizations prefer a 'big bang' approach with a major launch event raising awareness and provoking a spike in system use. Others prefer a lower-risk 'soft launch', with an emphasis on continued communication with stakeholders, while the model of 'perpetual beta' provides the opportunity to keep adapting the implementation indefinitely. The value and benefits of different types of launches are explored in more detail in Chapter 12.

Assess

In learning and development, assessment is synonymous with one of two things – checking knowledge and skills at the end of a course, or assessing the impact of learning, which is how we use it here. How do you assess the impact of learning? Plenty has been said and written in answer to this question, and many methodologies proposed, including the Kirkpatrick 4-level model of training evaluation, Jack Phillips' ROI Methodology and the Brinkerhoff Success Case Method.

In Chapter 9 we look at these methods, but (as the proponents of these methods would agree) there is only one ultimate test for the success of any learning programme or learning technology implementation: did it meet its stated business goal effectively and efficiently? To assess that requires three things – gathering evidence, assessing it against project aims and reporting on the results, whether these are in terms of hard money impacts or softer measures such as increased employee satisfaction.

Gathering information

Gathering information to check on the impact of an implementation cannot be done haphazardly, nor can it be done as an afterthought. In fact, gathering baseline data for the impact of an implementation should start at step 1, with understanding the project's aims in communication with stakeholders.

Assessing against project aims

When success is a matter of hard, quantifiable data, assessment is a clear process. Is the sales team selling more? Are the customer satisfaction ratings up? Even in these circumstances, though, isolating the effects of the technology from other factors is not easy. When success is measured less tangibly, both collecting the data and interpreting it is more difficult. This is why establishing upfront the stakeholders' perception of success is so important. Chapter 9 is dedicated to exploring this.

Reporting

Too often the L&D function ignores the need to report on the results of impact assessment, regarding it either as an internal measure of success or a weapon to be used in self-defence should the implementation be questioned. In fact, of course, reporting is essential and should form part of the team's regular communication with stakeholders. It affects not only the perception of this particular learning technology implementation, but also the overall perception of the department over the course of the project and in the future.

Sustain

The Sustain step is the final phase of an implementation, too often unloved and neglected. Here, the novelty is gone. There is no exciting technology to roll out, nothing new to reveal. Everything is in place, and the emphasis of work shifts for L&D. Up to this point, the team had to identify a business need, choose the right technology and implement it as *effectively* as possible to meet that need.

In the Sustain step, all this has been done. With the technology implemented, what remains is less dramatic than during the implementation step, but certainly as important. It is to make the technology work as well as possible within the boundaries that have been set. Given the aims, the technology and the employees using the system, how can the implementation's *efficiency* be improved?

Efficiency has something of a bad name in L&D, and with good reason. As we saw in Part One, too much of the profession's work – especially in this technological era – has concentrated on e-enabling things that should never have been done in the first place. The classic example of this is repeated attempts to make lectures available over the phonograph, the radio, the television or the internet, ignoring the fact that lectures are a poor method for transferring knowledge and even worse for building skills. All this is summed up in Peter Drucker's justly celebrated quote: 'There is nothing quite so useless as doing with great efficiency something that should not be done at all.' (Drucker, 1963)

This is why steps 1–5 are so important – they are all about deciding what *should* be done, and doing it well, so that the final step of sustaining the work can be taken in the sure knowledge that the implementation is worth improving.

This honing is best done using the Deming/Shewhart Plan-Do-Check-Act cycle, or some variation of it. Some L&D teams would claim that they never make it to this stage, that their implementations are in perpetual beta (see *Waterfall or agile?* above). I would argue that in most of these cases, the bulk of the implementation has been done, and what teams often call 'perpetual beta' is actually a very realistic understanding that the Sustain step is crucial, and never-ending.

While it is necessary to maintain, sustain and improve the implementation, this absolutely does not mean shouldering the burden of keeping a poorly implemented system running. Effort here is well spent if it includes a continued programme of gathering feedback and adjusting or tweaking a system to ensure continued relevance. Badly deployed effort includes time spent on manually transferring data from one system to another (typically done with Excel or CSV files), creating workarounds for parts of the implementation that don't quite work properly, or dealing with uncooperative vendors.

Finally, it is worth considering who should be in charge of sustaining the system. We will see in Chapter 10 that Herman Miller transferred the responsibility for the maintenance of its Electronic Performance Support System from the L&D function to the operational team closest to those using the system. The reason: they understood the immediate performance issues better than L&D and could respond to them faster.

The Partnership Principle

In each of the six steps in this model, L&D has to work with others. Initially, this is principally to understand the issues to be tackled. Later, L&D has to work with others again in the actual course of rolling the technology out. Finally, when sustaining the implementation, it once again has to work with the business – leaders, managers and employees – in understanding how the implementation can be improved. This is what I call the Partnership Principle, of working with others both within the organization and outside it.

The Partnership Principle is a reflection of two simple truths. One is that the L&D department is not expert in the running of the organization. This is not a value judgement, just a simple matter of fact. However well-versed it might be in the general rules of business, and however familiar with the overall aims of the organization, it does not know the detail of daily operations nor the full complexity of strategy. And yet an organizational learning technology implementation is only of any use if it serves the business and reflects these things. To fully understand the issues that need addressing, the L&D department must work in partnership with leaders, managers and employees. If it does not, any success in implementation will be a matter of chance rather than of good planning.

The other truth is that the Learning and Development department does not have all the skills needed to implement most learning technologies. Whether in IT, project management, marketing or other of the myriad skills needed, no single department can hope to house, under one roof, every skill required to implement all but the simplest of learning technology implementations. The other skills will need to be begged, borrowed and otherwise acquired by working with others inside and outside the organization.

Together, these two truths mean that learning technology implementations rely on partnership for their success as much as they rely on process. A methodology such as the 6-Step Process outlined here is certainly necessary to succeed in a learning technology implementation, but it is not sufficient. Success also relies on the implementation team having the right characteristics, one of the most obvious manifestations of which is a propensity for the team to partner with the rest of the organization rather than to work in isolation. This propensity is the result of a combination of four things – having a clear aim for the project, working with a focus on people, having a wide perspective on the implementation and, finally, having the right attitude. It is now time to turn our attention to these four characteristics of a learning technologies implementation and to meet some of the teams that have shown them.

Key takeaways

1 There are many good models for both organizational change and the process of implementing technology. Implementing a learning technology falls between these, as it both requires technical accuracy and must deal with cultural issues.

2 The 6-Step Process model suggested in this chapter begins with the necessity of understanding the business, political and technical aspects of the implementation.

3 The first part of planning the implementation consists of recruiting the right team to ensure it has the full set of skills for success, including project management and communications skills as well as the required technical skills.

4 Testing does not simply mean testing that the implementation works technically. It also means testing process impact and usability.

5 In the implementation step, it is essential that the communications plan be begun before the technology piece.

6 Assessment of impact can be done by a variety of methodologies, but they all rely on having initially correctly identified the key business driver for the project.

7 The Test-Implement-Assess steps may take place once, or in successive iterations.

8 The final step is to Sustain the implementation. This may be done by the L&D department alone, or it may be carried out in partnership with other departments.

9 This 6-Step Process will only succeed if the L&D department works in partnership with the rest of the organization.

References

APM (2014) *Factors in Project Success*, Association for Project Management, Princes Risborough

Drucker, P (1963) [accessed 11 December 2016] Managing for Business Effectiveness, *Harvard Business Review*, May, Boston, [Online] https://hbr.org/1963/05/managing-for-business-effectiveness

Franklin, M (2011) *Managing Business Transformation, A Practical Guide*, IT Governance Publishing, London

Gawande, A (2011) *The Checklist Manifesto: How to get things right*, Profile Books, London

Hamel, G and Zanini, M (2014) [accessed 11 December 2016] Build a Change Platform, Not a Change Program, *McKinsey & Company*, October, [Online] http://www.mckinsey.com/business-functions/organization/our-insights/build-a-change-platform-not-a-change-program

Imai, M (1986) *Kaizen: The key to Japan's competitive success*, Random House Business Division, New York

Ishikawa, K (1985) *What is Total Quality Control? The Japanese Way*, Translated by David J Lu, Prentice-Hall, Englewood Cliffs

Kotter, J P (1996) *Leading Change*, Harvard Business School Press, Boston

Kotter International (2014) [accessed 11 December 2016] 8-Step Process, *Kotter International*, [Online] http://www.kotterinternational.com/the-8-step-process-for-leading-change/

Lewin, K (1947) Frontiers in Group Dynamics: Concept, method and reality in social science; social equilibria and social change, *Human Relations*, **1** (1), pp 5–41

Shewhart, W A and Deming, E W (1987) *Statistical Method from the Viewpoint of Quality Control*, Dover Publications, New York

APPA: Four characteristics of success

08

Rules are mostly made to be broken and are too often for the lazy to hide behind. GENERAL DOUGLAS MACARTHUR

A good model is essential to the success of any change programme. However, models – including my own suggested six steps – carry an inherent risk. Precisely because they are necessary for success, it is tempting to believe that they are sufficient for it. They are not. Following a model unquestioningly is potentially catastrophic. When that happens, the model ceases to be a tool in the service of change and becomes instead its driver.

The problem is that a model, or any description of a process, can only imperfectly capture the nuances and complexities of a technology implementation. As Alfred Korzybski noted, the map is not the territory. Any description of a process highlights the key features, the salient points, the aspects of the geography of change we most need to be aware of. It cannot, however, provide the detail of conditions on the ground. That will be unique to each situation, and can only be experienced first-hand.

When someone implements a technology for the first time, the lack of previous experience can provoke a reaction – a too-rigid application of a model can lead to what General MacArthur described in the quote at the beginning of this chapter. The rules become a cover to hide behind. They provide an unfounded sense of certainty and security that is at best misleading in the complex world of organizational adult learning.

While it is crucial, therefore, for learning and development professionals to use a model of change and to develop a clear plan for the adoption of the technology they plan to implement, this is not enough to guarantee success and it is negligent to assume that it is. In my observation, the individuals and teams who successfully implement learning technologies, in addition to using a model, exhibit four common characteristics.

First, they all have a clear *aim*. This aim is expressed in practical terms; this implementation will solve a particular business problem. We would expect as much from the first stage of any of the models mentioned, whether it is the 'understand' or the 'discovery' phase. With successful implementations, however, the purpose is often couched in an understanding of the wider values and longer-term aims of the company – the implementation is seen as a coherent part of a larger plan.

Second, they know that a technology implementation depends on people: the employees, the people on the learning implementation team, the vendors and implementation partners and the managers and executives of the organization. Any implementation lacking the active support and participation of these people will be a pointless failure. Successful learning technology implementers recognize this and have a strong *people focus*.

Third, those who have made a success of their learning technology implementation consistently reveal a sense of *perspective* that goes beyond the immediate realm of this particular implementation. They know how this particular piece of work fits in. They know how things work internally in their organization, what is important, where to go to get things done and how things are likely to change in the future. But they also carry out what British organizational learning expert Nigel Paine calls horizon scanning, gleaning information from a range of sources to understand how both learning technologies and the business itself are likely to change in coming years. This helps them not only formulate and present their case for implementation, but also to plan it coherently and prevent it being rendered redundant in the future.

Finally, successful learning technology implementers above all have a pragmatic *attitude*. They make good calls on those decisions where the rules cannot help, or might deliver a poor outcome. They are prepared to compromise to deliver an effective solution today rather than a perfect one tomorrow. Usually, this pragmatism has its roots in a combination of experience with the company, a certain understanding of what makes people tick, and good common sense. Frequently, although not always, the most pragmatic individuals are those who have a wide experience at work.

Whether an organization is implementing a complex learning management system for an international audience or the simplest of cloud-based tools for use in a single office, if the implementation is successful, the people responsible for it exhibit APPA: a clear *aim*, a focus on *people*, a wide *perspective* in and beyond the organization and a pragmatic *attitude*. The rest of Part Two – the core of this book – is dedicated to examining these characteristics in more detail and exploring the tools and techniques to develop these characteristics.

An APPA implementation: The Hershey Company

When The Hershey Company successfully rolled out an LMS to 11,000 employees worldwide in 2015, the HR function displayed APPA in good measure. Headquartered in Hershey, Pennsylvania, United States, the chocolate confectionery company had 17 plants worldwide at the time of implementation, including operations in the United States, Mexico, India, Brazil and Canada. It manufactures, markets and distributes products under more than 80 brand names to approximately 70 countries.

The complexity of Hershey's operations are intensified by the range of languages spoken and the spread of employees over territories and time zones, not to mention that the workforce is split roughly 35:65 between salaried employees and hourly production employees. The former tend to be office workers, with computers and internet access, the latter typically are manufacturing employees with limited access to IT at work.

According to Megan Garrett, the Manager of Enterprise Learning, it was the company's plan to expand operations into Malaysia that precipitated the need for an enterprise-wide learning management system.

Megan had already been with the company for 16 years when this expansion was suggested. One of her first roles when she joined the company in 1999 had been supporting the implementation of the company's first learning management system. It was very costly and cumbersome to administer, and when the option came up to renew the licence three years later, the company declined.

Instead, they managed the marketing, delivery, registration and tracking of courses via an ingenious, home-grown solution combining a series of different technologies, not all of them designed for handling learning. Employees saw a single interface for all e-learning and class-room courses, and found the system straightforward to use. Behind the scenes, however, the system had grown increasingly complex over time, so that by 2015 it required – in Megan's estimation – 50 different steps to register an individual for a class. This, in her words, 'bubble gum and popsicle stick methodology' involved a considerable amount of manual intervention, including the inevitable manipulating of data in Excel spreadsheets, to ensure a smooth operation.

For some in this position, the idea that the Learning and Development department would shortly have the additional responsibility of training an entirely new workforce in a plant on the other side of the world might have seemed like a step too far. For Hershey's L&D team, it was the opportunity they had been looking for to create the training programme of the future in a high-tech new-build plant. And clearly the only way to train a large number of new employees rapidly and allow production to begin on time was to use e-learning.

In April 2015, together with her manager, Mary Farrell, and two counterparts from the IS (Information Systems) team, Megan created a business case, which was presented to the Senior Vice President of Global Operations and a number of VPs. After consideration, a number of meetings and implementation partner assessment, HR received the green light to purchase and implement an LMS in November.

Establishing the need and aim

The immediate need of the LMS was clear. It would enable Hershey to ensure that staff in the new plant were well trained in time for operations to begin. There was also, though, another goal, a larger purpose. Implementing an LMS across the organization would allow for countless small efficiency improvements in L&D operations, greater reliability by abandoning the manually intensive system and ensure worldwide consistency in operations. It would also make it possible for the HR team to support any further expansion without adding headcount. As we will see, the implementation of a learning technology often has two aims like this – an explicit, immediate one, with a clear, tangible benefit, and a larger one, widely regarded as important; but, seldom justified by any short-term financial measure.

In this case, as usual, the immediate aim was the ticket to the larger one. No L&D team in any company has ever had a major expense signed off on the basis that it would improve the department's internal operations, especially when these, although burdensome, have been working fine for the previous 16 years. Megan was sure the Senior Vice President of Global Operations would be sympathetic to the request, but also knew that, of course, he had a financial responsibility to the company. The LMS would have to pay its way.

The clearest way in which the LMS could justify itself was risk mitigation. A company manufacturing internationally has a swathe of employment, food and safety regulations to meet. Megan worked with the Legal Department to create a business case around the financial impact of non-compliance. What was the typical cost of lawsuits in their sector? Megan was able to establish that in terms of legal risk mitigation alone, the LMS was a worthwhile investment. Of course, the executive team recognized the need to have fully trained personnel, but processes and systems in place were already taking care of that. The risk around extending the existing training methods to Malaysia was more difficult to define. In contrast, the legal risk was very clear and justified the investment.

There is nothing extraordinary about pitching investment in an LMS (or any training-tracking technology) as a way of mitigating risk. What makes it important here is that – although valid as a justification for purchasing the LMS – it was not the initial aim. Megan's ability to understand how to pitch the LMS was a matter of understanding the wider perspective of the organization. She knew whom to approach internally to establish whether the legal rationale was a good one, and so she was able to establish a clear organizational purpose for the implementation. It was a very pragmatic approach.

Networks, stakeholders and resisters

Knowing who can affect an implementation both positively and negatively is an essential part of an implementation. So, too, is a network of contacts that will provide external validation of plans, and which will be able to act as a critical friend towards them. Usually, those behind successful implementations have these networks in place. Occasionally, they are skilled networkers who can create the network from scratch in short order.

This people focus is crucial because it is an organization's people for whom learning technology is implemented, and it is the people who will ultimately decide whether it succeeds or fails. Once the aim of an implementation is established, it is crucial to follow with a stakeholder analysis that combines a people focus with a clear perspective on the organization. In Megan's stakeholder analysis, her team identified multiple groups which could affect and be affected by the implementation. These included segments of the employees, the leadership population, helpdesk and client support, and two critical groups – training administrators in plant locations across the business and those employees currently delivering training and creating training materials.

The training administrators would be most affected by changes, but for them the impact would be largely positive. Although their work would change considerably, it would be mostly a matter of becoming familiar with a new, more effective system. Approximately 50 people across the business creating courseware, however, could possibly be resistant to change. They were involved in creating or adjusting training materials to fit local circumstances, but the central Learning and Development department saw the need for a coherent, well-branded and limited set of compliance training courses, for example on safety that could deliver a consistent message across the business.

Recognizing that these training staff were positive about the implementation but might want to retain their role of producing courses locally, Megan began communicating with them well before she received approval for the LMS purchase. The pitch was made in April, and immediately afterwards, she began a conversation with this extended group of training professionals. Approval for the LMS purchase was not received until November 2014, and thanks to these months of two-way communication, Megan was able to get the training staff on board, keep them positive about the implementation, and help them realize that there would be plenty of creative work to do following the go live… it would just be different.

In many large-scale implementations, one of the key stakeholder groups affected – and one which can have a significant influence on success – is the distributed personnel supporting learning across the organization. Bring them on board and they can be champions. Ignore them at your peril.

If stakeholder analysis is best done by combining the organizational perspective with a strong people focus, the implementation phase is a matter for informed pragmatism supporting the overall purpose. Any software system can be used as it is, out of the box. This seldom supports the full aim of the organization, so the system can usually be configured (making changes as part of the system) or customized (writing new code to solve a particular issue – almost always a chargeable service). The aim is always to reduce customization to a minimum, lowering both the time taken for implementation and the cost of delivery. Ideally, the out-of-the-box solution should be a good start – perhaps getting you 80 per cent of the way to your ideal solution. Closing the gap on the remaining 20 per cent on time and within budget is a matter of understanding what is essential, what is useful and what is nice to have. That can only be decided by working with the people in the business, and understanding the processes likely to be affected.

Implementation and process impact

With an LMS, the impact on processes is always likely to be large. E-learning courses and resources need to be made available internally, usage often needs to be tracked, assessments need to be run, stored, and the results made available to HR and managers. With an organization as widespread as Hershey, you could expect the number of different processes to be significant, and you would be right.

How do you identify exactly what the learning administration processes are before you implement a technology that may alter them? Hershey did this by creating a flowchart describing the individual processes for creating, advertising and managing courses. In total there were nine processes, and each took place across 23 different groups. These groups were in some cases defined by territory, others were functions or individual plants. Each had its own particular requirements and in each group there was a possibility that the processes would vary. The process flowchart mapped all of these possibilities – a 9×23 grid containing 207 cells, all potentially different.

For an LMS implementation, creating a process flow is essential. But, to return to General MacArthur's words at the beginning of this chapter, rules are not things to hide behind. Once the processes have been defined, questions need to be answered: do we need all these processes? Can we simplify some? How much is the variation a matter of culture, or simply of habit, and how much is it an essential part of the way work is done in a particular place? Usually there are no simple answers to these questions; rather the answers have to be formulated in discussion. In these discussions with stakeholders, the process flowchart is a key tool. It helps keep conversation on track and focused, making it possible to make informed, pragmatic decisions. The result of this conversation at Hershey – as with most LMS implementations – was the configuration workbook for the system. Creating this is one of the hardest, most time-consuming parts of the job of implementing an LMS. However, if that step is missed, there might be implications down the line as each department attempts to accommodate its particular processes to the LMS. Alternatively, there is risk that they could abandon it, instead using the familiar, pre-implementation systems.

The importance of the team

It is in these sorts of discussions that having the right team together really pays dividends. We will look at the make-up of an implementation team in a later chapter, but suffice to say that any significant implementation is always a team effort. Megan's core team consisted of five people: her manager, two people from the IS function, and a project manager. Megan describes the role of the project manager as absolutely essential for keeping the project on time and the team focused on deliverables. Particularly in the depths of the implementation phase, when difficult decisions have to be made, that project management discipline is essential.

While every roll-out needs a core team, that team also relies on close advisors. With a large technology implementation, the team will need to work closely with the vendor or an implementation partner who knows the software inside out. For Hershey, their implementation partner was an international technology company. Megan describes their knowledge of the platform as invaluable in helping make the right choices and technical decisions. Part of the role of such organizations is to help advise where processes can be supported using existing functionality. If change is necessary, they also make the change through configuration rather than more costly customization.

One simple example of this for Hershey was how users would search for courses. Crucial for a geographically dispersed organization, Hershey wanted to be able to search by location. The platform was not able to do this, but it could store courses by delivery method in two different fields. Megan had one of the delivery method fields for subject area reassigned. Instead, it now referred to location, and the filter enabled users to find courses according to their locale. This is a classic example of a small change to accommodate an existing process rather than cut costly new code.

Top-level support

Megan's main strategic input and support came from the LMS Steering Committee that she set up. Made up of 13 executives representative of functions across the enterprise, the steering committee provided unique perspective from each business unit and helped guide the team's decision-making. Although not everyone could attend physically, the hour-long meetings were run as a physical event at Hershey's headquarters with remote members dialling in from around the globe.

Hershey's LMS steering committee provided strategic insight as well as practical guidance. For example, the LMS allows employees to log external training not provided by the system. If they attend a conference or a course, they can add that to their profile. Originally, the L&D team had set this up to require manager approval. The steering committee's reaction was that this was unnecessary. They trusted their employees, and didn't need to burden managers with this. Over the months of the project, a series of small decisions like this can make a huge difference to how the implementation is finally received.

Pre-read information prepared by Megan ensured all members of the LMS steering committee were fully briefed in advance, but follow-up was also significant. The minutes of the steering committee were also shared with the HR leadership team, so that all HR VPs were fully informed about strategic discussions and decisions.

Building and maintaining those connections with the HR community are essential pre-launch, during implementation and post-launch. The go-live date was set as seven months after the decision to purchase. In the build-up to launch, Megan was keen to keep communications open at all levels to understand how stakeholders would react to the system – its proposed configurations, the look and feel and any process changes. One key stakeholder group that she was regularly in touch with was the HR Business Partners, which consisted of the HR managers from each function across the business.

Nigel Paine refers to committees and groups like these as providing 'air cover' for an implementation. The greater the number of people affected by what is happening, the more important this sort of high-level support is. Knowing it would be crucial, Megan set up the LMS Steering Committee immediately following the decision to purchase. First gaining the assent of her VP, she made all the contacts herself via e-mail, explaining the importance of the committee, how it would run and made clear that the demands on members would be limited.

This proactive approach to the implementation illustrates one side of the crucial attitude behind a successful implementation: a propensity for action. The other side of the pragmatic attitude that underlies success with these implementations is shown in the grinding work of creating the process map and using it to create the vital LMS configuration workbook.

Demonstrating APPA

During its award-winning LMS implementation, The Hershey Company exhibited APPA from the start by working with stakeholders to establish a clear aim that resonated with the business, while maintaining a subsidiary – and much needed – aim of improving internal procedures technically within the L&D function, especially around supporting online training internationally.

People focus was apparent in several areas. First, there was the choice of team members, where Megan picked a team that would balance and complement her own skillset – including, for example, an experienced project manager on the team. The team's communications were also comprehensive, from ensuring distributed personnel responsible for L&D were brought on board even before the project was approved, to regularly briefing and receiving feedback from a range of senior personnel and HR directors and managers.

The composition of the team ensured a wider perspective within the organization by including staff from outside L&D. Team leader Megan Garrett brought her own, wider understanding of Hershey to the team, having worked for the company for 16 years and built up a considerable network over that time. In addition, the team's perspective on business issues was informed by feedback from the senior groups they reported to.

The attitude that drives a successful learning technology implementation is most characteristically seen in a single-minded pursuit of the agreed aim, combined with the ability to negotiate and compromise on the way. One place the Hershey team showed this was in the detailed work done on the process flowchart. Striving for perfection in each of the 207 cells on the spreadsheet would have left the project off-track and floundering, while rushing through the process would have created serious problems later on. What they achieved was the optimal result, which is what attitude is really all about – driving the project on so that it is finished well, on time and within budget.

Ensuring the four characteristics

We will examine these four factors in the succeeding chapters of this book, illustrating each with one or more case studies and exploring how to build them into an implementation. These four characteristics can all be developed in a team, but when doing so, it is worth considering an important distinction between the first two and the last two.

The first two – a clear aim and a focus on people – can both be described in terms of activity. Arriving at the aim of the project is a matter of working well with key decision makers, both to understand the goals of the business and to describe the implementation in terms that reflect those goals. It is, as we will explore in the next chapter, a matter of how to reach a consensus on value and express it clearly. It is also a matter of knowing how to carry out a useful conversation, using the skills of performance consulting and good listening as well as using a sense of political awareness.

Any good learning technology implementation has to be focused on the people involved, through techniques such as including stakeholder management and communications planning, but also the matters of team selection and gathering feedback before, during and after the roll out. Like articulating the project aim, these are all things that can be described in terms of activity and which can be improved with the right tools and methods. The first two characteristics could be described, then, as skills-based.

In contrast, while the effects of perspective and attitude also show themselves in certain activities, these are the manifestations of a certain mindset. A team that seeks a wider perspective is constantly challenging itself to understand more about the broader context in which it works. It will explore L&D beyond its own practice, and it will examine the world of business, both inside the organization and beyond it. It will aim to learn from experience and have mechanisms for doing so. Yet although it will have these and other methods that create a wider perspective, the entire characteristic is the result of a particular mindset typified by two things: curiosity and a quest for improvement.

Similarly, a team with the right attitude gets things done through various methods such as well-planned projects and good meeting management, but behind those activities again is a mindset – a tendency towards taking action and completing things. These enable a team with the right attitude to overcome that seeming contradiction of relentlessly driving towards the implementation aim while at the same time being ready to compromise along the way. The mindset here is clear: the aim is so important that it is worth negotiating to reach it, rather than holding out for a perfect solution, which it never succeeds in attaining.

And the aim of the implementation is all-important. It is the focal point of the entire project, what makes it worthwhile, and where we start our exploration of APPA in detail.

Key takeaways

1 As well as following a process during implementation, successful learning technology implementation teams also typically exhibit APPA: an *aim*, a *people focus*, a wide *perspective*, and a pragmatic *attitude*.

2 During its award-winning LMS implementation, The Hershey Company exhibited APPA throughout its implementation.

3 An implementation aim will always need to have value for the executives signing it off. It may, however, have additional benefits, too.

4 Good implementations show their people focus in a range of ways, from team selection to the range of stakeholders consulted, to the effectiveness of communication and feedback generation during the project.

5 Perspective is a matter of knowing the world outside the immediate confines of L&D and of the business.

6 The attitude that drives successful implementations is most obviously seen in the team's bias towards action and completion.

7 While the Aim and People focus characteristics can be developed as skills, the right Perspective and Attitude are the manifestations of a mindset. All four characteristics, however, can be developed.

Aim

09

Learning occurs when an organization achieves what it intended; that is, there is a match between its design for action and the actual outcome. CHRIS ARGYRIS (1982) AS CITED IN 'CHRIS ARGYRIS: THE MANAGER'S ACADEMIC' IN *BUSINESS* (2003), P 965

Chris Argyris was an American business theorist, Professor Emeritus at Harvard Business School and author of the seminal *On Organizational Learning* and other key works. Argyris examined how organizations learned from their mistakes or failed to. Although he was not concerned in this book with the detail of implementing learning technologies, his observation of what makes for success at the highest level of organizational learning holds true for us: that learning occurs when 'there is a match between its design for action and the actual outcome'.

This match is, far too often, missing in learning technology implementations. Far too often the implementation fails because the initial step of understanding the needs of the organization is ignored or carried out inadequately. With no guide to the right outcome, the success of any action becomes a matter of chance. In contrast, implementations that work well always involve a degree of initial work consulting with the organization. The same is – perhaps unsurprisingly – true for any successful L&D work that goes beyond the transactional.

Is this initial consulting always necessary? In this book I largely make the assumption that the L&D department is leading the charge on selecting and driving the implementation of a particular learning technology. When that happens, I would expect the department to consult with the rest of the organization before spending its money, and most of this chapter explores the nature of how consultancy may be used to establish and measure the value that the implementation will provide.

Sometimes, however, the L&D department has no say in the implementation of a learning system. It may be that the organization has invested in a substantial ERP (Enterprise Resource Planning) platform such as Oracle, SAP or Infor, all of which include an LMS. In such cases, it is common, and understandable, for the finance or IT departments to require the use of the corporate LMS and forbid spend on anything else. The system is regarded as part of corporate infrastructure. Alternatively, it may be that the organization was the subject of an acquisition, and suffered the imposition of the learning technologies of the buying company. These are just two of many scenarios in which the L&D department can find itself removed from the decision of buying a particular technology. It would be a mistake, however, to assume this distance from decision-making means there is no need to engage with the business and to understand its needs. It is the role of L&D to know enough about the organization to understand where it can add value. From the detail of designing a 10-minute e-learning module, to the implementation of the most complex learning system, all activity should fit into a broad sense of where the organizational pain points are.

Consulting to establish the aim of a learning technology is not about justifying its purchase, although it may be used for that effect. It is about ensuring the technology is well implemented, and used effectively for the greatest benefit of the organization.

The ideal and the reality

Ideally, the beginning of any enterprise technology implementation follows a predictable series of stages, something like this, which would precede the first stage of most of the implementation processes covered in Chapter 7, and also encompass some of it:

1 Identification of a business problem.

2 Uncovering the causes behind this problem.

3 Finding the best solution for tackling the causes.

4 Pitching that solution to decision makers.

5 Begin implementation process.

Sometimes things actually go this way. As we saw, Hershey's needed to be sure that training was delivered consistently, and on time, to support new facilities in Malaysia. There was a clear business problem – the new staff needed to be trained and to the right standard. The cause was pretty clear: a new facility was opening. Megan Garrett made the pitch, got the green light and, together with her team and the support of an implementation partner, got to work.

Even with this implementation, however, the story was a little more complex, as we saw. The business problem was clear, but Megan chose to take a different angle when making her pitch. Rather than lead with the need for more consistent training, her pitch focused on the legal impact of failing to meet compliance regulations, also a legitimate outcome, but one which – importantly – could be measured in tangible dollar terms. In addition there was a third benefit: the additional tightening up and systemization of the training department's delivery procedures. Although valuable, this was seen as an ancillary benefit.

A learning technology implementation, then, may be associated with clear, measurable gains. It may also be associated with less tangible benefits, and there may be additional benefits that, while valuable or even essential, are not explicitly given as a justification for the implementation.

Examining case studies of learning technologies implementations over the past 16 years has convinced me that they seldom follow the idealized journey of technology-as-solution outlined above. Often the implementation takes place for other reasons, but is then cast in the light of technology-as-solution to meet expectations when telling the story after the event. Considering this 16-year range of uses of learning technologies, it appears to me that there are four types of implementation, each with a different aim. Some fit the model of technology-as-solution more easily than others. In order of increasing strategic consideration, the four types are:

Type 1. Organizational infrastructure – part of business as usual.

Type 2. More efficient L&D – doing existing L&D activity better.

Type 3. More effective learning – doing new L&D activity well.

Type 4. Part of organizational change – shifting the entire enterprise.

Type 1 implementations may be focused on business as usual, but they carry with them some important considerations. To set the scene for discussing organizational infrastructure implementations we will first consider the other three types.

The majority of implementations are probably type 2, focused on more efficient L&D delivery. They support the existing ways of training delivery in the organization. Typical measures of value for these implementations include: cost savings, reduced administration and shorter timescales to produce and distribute courses. Type 2 implementations do not explicitly aim to alter ways of learning, although this does sometimes happen organically. For example, webinars may be introduced in a move to place classroom-based instructor-led training online. Subsequently, employees may well discover that they can use the same technology themselves, with or without the L&D department, to have meetings, discuss performance issues and processes. During the course of these meetings they may well bring out the tacit knowledge of company experts, so making it explicit. Spreading this information among the meeting participants, and curating it for future reference by recording the meetings are excellent ways of supporting learning in new ways, and a result – albeit unintentional – of the original implementation.

Type 3 implementations – which set out to improve the effectiveness of learning – are less common. Whereas efficiency-focused implementations can usually be justified on the basis of contribution to the bottom line (for example through cost saving, risk avoidance or faster processes), it is generally harder to prove that learning more effectively has an impact on performance. This not so much because the techniques do not exist to prove it (as we will see later) but because it is usually difficult to isolate the effect of learning among a range of contributing causes to improved performance. In addition, making the case for a type 3 implementation is especially difficult for the L&D department if the rest of the organization suffers from the schoolroom assumption and believes that learning is synonymous with being taught in a course, and nothing else.

One area in which L&D departments can make a good case for a type 3 implementation is where it will ensure faster speed to competence and/or better retention, both of which are measurable. A classic example of this is Duolingo, the free language-learning app, which provides short daily bursts of learning activity delivered to a mobile phone or other smart device. Learning, being reminded of, and practising the use of, key information over time in this way is far more effective than the traditional approach of receiving a large lump of new information all at once – the classic classroom experience. Almost always, retention of new information delivered in a large, single load, rapidly declines down what is known as the 'Ebbinghaus Forgetting Curve' after 19th-century German experimental psychologist Hermann Ebbinghaus. In contrast, 'spaced learning' over time is more effective. As Dr Will Thalheimer notes in a meticulously researched paper, 'research shows that spacing learning over time produces substantial learning benefits' (Thalheimer, 2006). In recent years there has been a surge in systems similar to Duolingo, designed for the corporate market. Their growth is based on a proven record of enabling employees to learn essential information better, and usually faster and more cost-effectively. For a distributed workforce – for example a retail sales force spread across stores nationally, or pharmaceutical reps – it is possible to make a strong case for a type 3 implementation using this approach.

If it is often difficult for the L&D department to argue the case for a learning technology on the basis that it will be a better way to learn, then it is almost impossible to do it for the fourth type – an implementation carried out explicitly to support a wider change in the organization, usually a cultural change. I have only seen these implementations approved when they have been initiated by the board, which is what you would expect as organizational change initiatives almost always start at the top. In such cases, members of the executive suite are already bought into the idea of learning as catalysing or supporting organizational change. They are not looking for any hard measures of success, because while these certainly exist in organizational transformation, the change programme will encompass a number of initiatives, making it impossible to ascribe behavioural impact to the learning/training component alone.

For HC-One, the need for culture change was paramount, and was driven by its executive team. The British company provides specialist care for older people. In 2011, it was created as part of the rescue of care homes formerly run by Southern Cross, which had suffered a widely publicized collapse (BBC, 2011). When HC-One took over the running of some 250 homes, with over 10,000 residents and 15,000 employees, many were suffering from low morale, with a real risk of an impact on the quality of care provision (Towards Maturity, 2013). As part of a general initiative to ensure high-quality care, the executive team gave the go ahead for a new approach to company-wide training. The aim was explicit: to 'move from a "culture of training for compliance" to a culture of "training for quality and kindness"', in line with the company's aim to provide care 'with kindness, thoughtfulness and respect'.

The *touch* programme went on to win multiple awards, including the Learning and Performance Institute's 2014 Chief Learning Officer of the Year award for Alison Innes-Farquhar, the company's Head of People and Organizational Development. Focusing on delivering content using the best medium for the learner, it sought to embed learning and changed behaviours, rather than simply provide training. *Touch* used a variety of different delivery mechanisms, with linked learning activities to ensure what employees learned was used in the workplace. As part of this, managers – always a key component in any training programme – had discussion cards to engage employees in considering what they had learned, and how to put it into practice in the context of the home they were working in.

This was indeed a learning technologies implementation, with good use of video and mobile delivery – still at the early stages of corporate learning adoption in 2012 – but the role of technology was a supporting one in what was a fully formed programme of learning, communications and cultural change that met the chairman's aim of revitalizing the company. *Touch's* high participation rates of over 90 per cent participation within seven months were highlighted in the Cavendish Review (Cavendish, 2013). More importantly, employees showed an average 10 per cent increase across Gallup's 12 measures of staff engagement – a significant increase – and managers overwhelmingly said the programme had improved competence, not just compliance scores, and was supporting the aim of the organization delivering 'the kindest care' (Towards Maturity, 2013). The implementation had met its aim.

But if the implementation worked, was that success sustained? It was. In 2016, HC-One recorded its one millionth completed learning event. Also in 2016, Skills for Care, the national body charged with creating a skilled adult social care workforce, recognized HC-One as a Centre of Excellence, one of only seven in the UK.

Perhaps most important, though, has been the reaction of staff. In their annual survey, HC-One colleagues are asked what is the best thing HC-One has done for them, in the last 12 months. The format of the answer is free text, not multiple choice, so employees can suggest whatever they like. For the past four years, one word has consistently appeared more frequently than any other in those answers: 'training'. It is a long way from the disgruntled view of Sally, dismally slogging through her compliance training in Starbucks.

Let us return now to the first type of learning technology implementation. In comparison with carrying out cultural change, adding to the organizational infrastructure may seem dull. By definition there is nothing new about it. It consists of things like risk avoidance, like ensuring compliance, essentially it is about supporting business as usual. In many ways it is a matter of following the crowd, doing what every other similar organization does. This may seem a poor reason for doing anything, but the opposite is true. Sometimes, following the crowd can be a perfectly rational way of guiding decision-making.

Everett Rogers' curve for the Innovation Adoption Lifecycle (Rogers, 2003) divides adopters into five populations: innovators, early adopters, early majority, late majority and laggards. Based on Rogers' post-war observation of farmers' adoption of hybrid grain in Iowa, the curve shows the sociology of adoption: the slow build up as an idea gains credibility, the surge as a majority of users come on board, then the tailing off as the final adopters accept it.

Some users (the innovators and early adopters) support an idea early, out of innate enthusiasm or because they have some special reason to believe it will succeed. Once they have done so and shown the technology to be viable, the early majority come on board. (Note: there is nothing automatic about this transition from early adopters to early majority, as Geoffrey Moore points outs in *Crossing the Chasm*

(Moore, 1998). Some technologies fail to move beyond the innovator stage.) Other adopters are more wary, but once (to their minds) the technology has been solidly proven, the late majority adopt it. Finally, and often grudgingly, the laggards take it up. This process has been observed with the adoption of hybrid grain, televisions and mobile phones. In these cases, following the crowd in the early or late majority or even as a laggard cannot be said to have been harmful. Rather, it can be a wise approach to see which technologies eventually prove themselves.

By adopting a blended, mobile approach to learning in 2012, HC-One were certainly ahead of the norm, and may even have been considered early adopters. These technologies are now mainstream. Deciding to use them now, when they have been shown to be useful, may be 'following the crowd', but it can also be considered good, common sense, when one considers potential learning technologies such as the virtual worlds of Second Life, which – in the words of Geoffrey Moore – failed to 'cross the chasm' to mainstream adoption and either withered away, or became a specialist tool in a niche.

There is a difference, however, between adopting something which has been proven to be useful, and simply following a fad. This distinction is particularly important when adopting enterprise-wide technologies. They can be complex to implement, and the impact (positive or negative) may not be apparent until sometime after roll out. Because technology is constantly changing, new releases of software, or entirely new systems are released, promoted and adopted before their worth is proven. Unsure of what is right for them, organizations too frequently jump on the latest bandwagon, regardless of whether a particular technology is right for them. This is not a new problem. David S Linthicum referred to it in his 1999 book *Enterprise Application Integration*. This is how he discusses the adoption of new enterprise software at the end of the last century (Linthicum, 1999):

> IT managers made many of their decisions based on their perception of the current technology market. For example, when the UNIX platforms were popular in the early 1990s, UNIX was placed in many enterprises, regardless of how well it fit. Today, the same is true of Windows NT.

Clearly, the installation of these systems has been a textbook example of 'management-by-magazine.' Rather than making sound, business-driven decisions, or evaluating all possible solutions, decisions were made to implement the 'coolest' technology.

An L&D practitioner with any experience will recognize this desire to implement the latest, coolest technology – in others, and in themselves. There are plenty of instances in every type of implementation where learning technologists have opted for a suboptimal technology because it was the latest thing, rather than because it was the best for the job.

While it is possible to choose the wrong technology in any type of implementation, however, it seems to be particularly common in type 1 implementations, because very often the choice here is made by a non-L&D manager, willingly succumbing to poorly informed influences. Many in L&D will recognize the perils of what Linthicum calls 'management-by-magazine', in which a manager – often from outside the department – decides to implement a particular technology because they have heard about it from a colleague or read about it in the latest glossy business magazine.

In this situation, technology is fetishized, made a goal in itself and this is when following the crowd is a particularly bad idea. Many companies followed the crowd in the late 1990s and early 2000s and implemented LMSs that were a poor choice for their organization. Seduced by the promise of massive cost savings – and under the schoolroom assumption that learning is equivalent to making information available – they bought into systems without really understanding them, and failed to implement them well.

This is a danger in type 1 implementations, then. Following the crowd fails as the driver for a learning technology implementation when it does not provide a well-articulated sense of value for the project. 'We'll use this technology, because it's been proven for our type of organization, because it will help us conduct our current business, and because we're confident its success can be measured against current business metrics' makes sense. 'We'll use this technology because everyone else is' is a recipe for disaster.

When properly conducted, the other types of implementation also all incorporate their own gauge of value. A type 2 implementation, focused on efficiency, by definition has clear measures of success – if it makes existing L&D practice better, it has succeeded. A type 3 implementation that seeks to improve the effectiveness of learning can also use existing metrics, such as reduced time to competence. A type 4 implementation may have metrics attached to it, too – HC-One's implementation was a success in terms of employee engagement and perceived improvement of care delivery. (It is important to note, though, that learning is only a contributor to these metrics. Management, coaching and other factors also played a role in improving them. It would be impossible to isolate learning's particular role in the shift.)

Type	Aim	Example metrics
Type 1	Organizational infrastructure	Effective business-as-usual, risk avoidance, compliance
Type 2	More efficient L&D delivery	Cost savings in L&D, reduced administration, faster delivery
Type 3	More effective learning	Faster time to competence, better retention
Type 4	Part of organizational change	Defined by the sponsors of change

In each of the four types of implementation the aim will be different, as will its measure. Whatever the aim and measure, however, they should be clear and determined in advance. Without them, there is no way of knowing whether the implementation has succeeded. The aim is a destination point. The measure of value associated with it lets everyone involved in the project know whether the destination has been successfully reached. For example, if the aim is to improve retail sales by helping the sales staff learn better using spaced learning delivered over mobile devices, then the metric is clearly: Did sales improve more than they might have done anyway given the time of year and background trends?

Not all success can be measured, however. Sometimes there is real value in achieving something through learning which has no metric attached to it.

This lack of a metric need not matter, provided that this non-measurable value is something thought to be important by the people responsible for the organization's success, and provided its effects can be seen. Suppose line managers have noticed that live online training seems to suffer because the trainers are culturally insensitive to employees from certain geographies: an online course to help the trainers be more culturally aware may well make the delivery more efficient. The impact of this would be difficult to measure, but would be palpable in the reaction of those being trained. If the line managers concerned are satisfied with this improved reaction, then that is an adequate measure of success. The same is true for the advantages of providing more background reading material online for a cadre of professional workers. The long-term impact of this is impossible to isolate, but if those workers' managers believe it to be useful, then it almost certainly is worth doing.

Type	Aim	Example non-measurable value
Type 1	Organizational infrastructure	Avoidance of reputational risk
Type 2	More efficient L&D delivery	Trainers more culturally aware
Type 3	More effective learning	Wider range of background professional content
Type 4	Part of organizational change	Defined by the sponsors of change

L&D professionals are often tempted to focus only on measurable value as the metric of success for a learning implementation, and to want to express it in monetary terms. While useful, finding the financial value of learning is no simple matter.

Hard value and the use, misuse and abuse of 'ROI'

The metric of the monetary impact of learning that L&D most often reaches for is 'Return on Investment', or ROI. This term is frequently used in making decisions at the executive level of organizations, as a way of understanding whether an investment will pay its way. For an organization planning to install some new equipment, the ROI calculation is clear: the plant will cost you something, and output will increase after installation. The ratio of that increase to the total cost of the new equipment is the ROI:

Return on Investment = incremental value / investment made

This should be expressed as a return over a period, and as a percentage. If the new piece of plant cost a total of £10,000 to buy and install, then that is the investment made. If it produces an extra £2,000 worth of value per year, that is the incremental value. It will, therefore, yield an ROI of 2,000/10,000, or 20 per cent, per year, meaning that after five years, the machinery will have paid for itself.

People, though, are not machines, and making the same calculation for training proves more complex. The first issue is simply to know the worth of an employee's output. For most office workers, this is difficult to calculate. They are not production line machines, the output of which has a specific value, and furthermore what they do produce (documents, ideas and so on) is usually part of a complex chain of production involving many people.

Even for employees whose output can be clearly measured, such as some manual workers and sales people, proving that any change in that output was the result only of training, is complicated. There is just too much else going on to easily isolate the effects of the training. Put it this way: if, after training, a group of employees shows an increase in productivity, is that down to the training? Not necessarily. The change might have been part of an ongoing trend, or might have happened anyway due to something else.

To be sure that the change would not have happened anyway, we need to know how that group of employees performed before training. Suppose they are sales people – were their sales at a flat level, or already on an upward path? If the latter, then did the training result in an increase in sales beyond the trend that already existed?

And a historical trend is not the only way an increase in performance can be caused by something other than training. Perhaps the employer made internal systems more efficient, or a competitor went bankrupt, reducing overall supply and making it easier for the sales people to sell. To see whether these factors caused any increase in productivity, we need to divide our sales force into two groups, with only one receiving training. This second group should be as similar as possible in every way to the trained group, from their age and educational background to their locations, experience and knowledge. And both groups need to be large enough in size – usually at least 30 people.

If we can set up a training group and a control group like this, and be sure what the historical productivity trend was, we can be fairly sure to identify any productivity increases stemming from training. I say fairly sure, because there is still the Hawthorne effect to consider, in which people increase productivity simply as a result of change or observation. (In the Western Electric Hawthorne electrical plant in the 1920s, workers' productivity increased temporarily when factory floor lighting was improved, and then increased again when it was reduced.) (Economist, 2008).

If the Hawthorne effect can be accounted for, and if we have historical data and a control group, then ROI should be calculable in instances where we can calculate the value of the work of the employees concerned.

So if it is possible to calculate the ROI for a learning intervention (and hence for the technology that supports it) why does it not happen more often? One reason is that if you want to implement an ROI study, it takes a lot of effort. An organization asked if they would like such a study will almost always reply 'No thanks, it's okay. We know the training's going to work anyway.' This is the response I received countless times when trying to produce an ROI study for my employer – a classroom IT training company – in the 1990s. The customers were already bought into the idea of training and saw the ROI study as superfluous, even if it was offered for free.

Similarly, it was only after several years of false starts that Neil Rackham, a scientifically rigorous research psychologist and founder of sales training company Huthwaite, was able to find an organization willing to undergo a rigorous ROI trial – Motorola, Canada.

The results (published in Appendix A of Rackham's 1988 book *SPIN Selling*) did indeed show a significant increase in sales as a result of training. Most trainers would regard them as sound. Most marketers would have jumped on them as proof positive of the impact of the SPIN Selling approach. However, the research scientist Rackham was less sure, writing in his book: 'There are even more tests I'd like to carry out before I'll be totally satisfied that the ideas I've described in this book will significantly improve the results of major sales' (Rackham, 1988).

Rackham stood to gain considerably by proclaiming the validity of the training programme he had devised. If he felt less than totally convinced by his ROI study, this is surely a lesson for the rest of us. ROI is complicated; done properly it is time consuming and it may not in the end be convincing to an expert in the field.

The misuse of ROI

In L&D, the term 'ROI' is often used to describe calculations that lack Rackham's scientific rigour. Most so-called ROI studies have no control group and no baseline data. Some simply describe cost savings.

One man that has attempted to provide rigour in calculating ROI in learning is Jack Phillips, who set up the ROI Institute for exactly this purpose. An article co-authored by Phillips, and available on the Institute's website bemoans the weakness of most claims to ROI in L&D:

> In a recent review of award-winning elearning and mobile learning case studies published by several prestigious organizations, not one project was evaluated at the ROI level where the monetary value of the impact was compared with the program's cost. *They used the concept of ROI to mean any value or benefit from the program.* [Emphasis mine] (ROI Institute, 2014)

As someone who regularly judges awards entries in the field myself, I can entirely corroborate this depressingly familiar story. This slap-dash approach to the use of a very precisely defined accounting term has exactly the opposite effect to what is intended. Rather than adding to the credibility of the user, it undermines it. Worse, it undermines the credibility of the profession they are associated with.

It is not impossible to run a rigorous ROI study; it just requires effort and a willing organization. Indeed, the quoted article, *ROI Calculations for Technology-Based Learning*, does go on to cite a case study of a properly conducted study. The programme concerned the use of a mobile learning application to train sales staff how to describe and sell an upgrade to a software product widely used in the trucking industry, ProfitPro. As this was a new product, there was no trend data. The study used a representative control group. The results were impressive: with increased speed to competence, the trained representatives made their first sale faster, and sold more per month, adding up to a 311 per cent ROI for the trained group. Among the additional, intangible benefits were: stress reduction for sales associates, customer satisfaction and enhanced company reputation.

For someone who feels passionately that L&D needs a clear understanding of what ROI really means, it is a pleasure to read about a well-conducted study. A proper study does, however, take time and effort to carry out, and there are alternatives.

'Impact' over 'ROI'?

Instead of an in-depth ROI study, it is possible to measure the impact of a learning programme using methods similar to, but less painstaking than, ROI.

Matt DeFeo is Senior VP for Sales, Training & Recruiting at Techtronic Industries (TTI) a multi-billion dollar, global power-tool company. Between 2010 and 2011, Matt introduced a simple e-learning programme supported by the corporate LMS. The programme's aim was to ensure that goods were only accepted for return within the terms of the company's warranty. The programme focused on the 10 most common ways returned power tools did not meet warranty requirements. Over two years the impact was a reduction in returns from 4 per cent to 1.8 per cent. A fall of 2.2 per cent may not sound like much, but for a company the size of TTI that amounts to a substantial saving – some US $33–35 million over two years with TTI's key customers. Against this, the four-year investment in the LMS, implementation and consultancy was less than US $1 million (Learning Technologies, 2012).

E-learning was not the sole cause of this impressive saving. After all, the programme involved management reinforcing the message and implementing the returns policy. Other factors may have been involved as well. There was no trend data (was the 4 per cent return rate rising or falling prior to the programme?) nor any control group. This view of impact, then, is less rigorous than a full ROI study, but practically speaking, it was undoubtedly sufficient. The training programme clearly played an important part in the change, and the change was – to say the least – significant.

Over the same period, Matt ran another programme, moving new product training online from face-to-face delivery. The aim here was not cost saving (although that was a side effect), it was increased effectiveness. Scheduling face-to-face courses meant that often products were launched before training could reach a dispersed sales force. Making the training available before product launch, online, to all sales people, meant they were able to start selling on average three months sooner than they had done with face-to-face training. Three months is a substantial proportion of the average five-year life of a power tool, Matt conservatively calculated this led to a 2 per cent increase in sales. Again, 2 per cent may not sound like much, but for an organization the size of TTI, it amounts to millions of dollars of impact, substantially more than the cost of developing the course and even of the LMS it ran on. Once again, there is no trend data or control group here, and there is no accounting for exogenous factors that might have caused sales to increase (although actually the increase took place during a building recession, when comparable companies' sales suffered). That degree of precision was not necessary. When it came to showing the results of training, both TTI's management and its L&D department were confident that the numbers were good enough to demonstrate a positive, cost-effective impact (CERTPOINT Systems, 2012).

Depending on the degree of rigour required, then, both ROI studies and impact studies are useful in showing the value of learning programmes and the technologies that support them. There are, however, caveats to bear in mind before using either.

The limits of numbers

The most obvious limitation of impact and ROI studies is that they can only be done after an implementation. In other words, while they can show that you achieved your aim, they cannot prove in advance that you will be successful. Having said that, the methods used in an

impact/ROI study can certainly be presented as a compelling hypotheti-
cal case. Suppose, prior to implementation, it had been suggested that
the ProfitPro mobile sales training system would show an ROI of say
150 per cent – in other words that it would more than pay for itself.
Showing the conservatively laid out figures, the thinking behind them,
and the predicted increase in sales would have gone some considerable
way towards making a persuasive case for giving the implementation
the go ahead. And then, when the figures were calculated after the
implementation, and the ROI found to be in excess of 300 per cent, the
stock of the L&D department would have risen considerably.

The ProfitPro study was a rigorous one. However, as I found with the
companies that I tried to convince to run ROI studies in the 1990s, very
often organizations simply do not want an ROI or impact study either
in advance or afterwards. For these organizations, the 'good enough'
calculation will suffice, as long as it is conservative and realistic. Very
often there is no need even to measure the exact cost of the implementation to the last penny or cent. The reason for this is that experienced
managers and executives know that apparent precision can often mask a
host of questionable assumptions; one simple example: when employees
are involved part time on the implementation, assessing the proportion
of their salary to allocate to implementation costs is always a judgement
call, not a matter of accounting. Using a conservative approximation is
often more credible than attempting and claiming total precision.

If senior managers or executives show an apparent lack of interest
in precise numbers, that does not mean that they think value cannot
or should not be measured in monetary terms. It means that they are
more concerned with credibility than precision. It also often means
that they may have an idea in their own minds of what value means
to them. We will shortly examine how to uncover that concept of
value, but first it is important to understand how the term 'ROI' is
sometimes, quite deliberately, abused by those in authority.

The abuse of ROI

Anyone who truly understands ROI calculations knows how thorough they are, and how much effort they are to complete. For
anybody wanting to delay anything new – a training programme, or

a technology implementation for example – asking for an ROI study, or indeed an in-depth impact study, is the perfect blocker to progress. It could take weeks to complete, and when it is presented, the detail can always be questioned. This is an abuse of the term 'ROI', and it is an abuse that occurs far too often.

When managers or executives take this approach, the problem is not that they need to be persuaded by some numbers. It is that they need to be fundamentally convinced that your project has any worth at all. Arguments making a case for training based on numbers involve a tacit assumption that these numbers matter to the organization and to the person concerned. For both TTI and the trucking software company the assumption was correct – more sales and fewer invalid returns were welcome. But most of what matters to an organization is not usually as clear cut, and L&D makes a basic error if assumes it knows what the issues are, without checking first.

Once the issues are established, and the value attached to them is clear, an impact or ROI study can always be used as supporting evidence, but the key thing is always to establish what is valuable to the key stakeholders in the first place. Doing this takes us out of the traditional and familiar area of L&D – being responsible for the creation and distribution of courses – and into the very different area of performance consulting.

Perceived value and performance consulting

Performance consulting is a blanket term for a range of methods of exploring the causes of below-standard performance and agreeing on ways of tackling them. Performance is sometimes described using this formula:

$$P = f(A, M, O)$$

This expresses the idea that performance (P) is a function of Ability, Motivation and Opportunity. It was popularized by Peter Boxall and John Purcell in their book *Strategy and Human Resource Management*. A sales person might be excellent at selling and know her entire product set, for example (Ability), she might have a compensation plan that keeps her focused on her task (Motivation), but it may be that the back office systems for processing orders are substandard, resulting in more returned returns and lower net sales (Opportunity) (Boxall and Purcell, 2002).

This formula suggests that when faced with a performance problem, managers and executives in an organization should consider which of these three variables needs to be addressed to improve performance. In our example, net sales will be best addressed by tackling the back office problems, not by providing our sales person with more product training or a new commission structure.

For L&D to consider performance in this way, and for it to consult internally to establish the root causes of poor performance is a major shift in the traditional role of the function. We will explore this shift more fully in Part Three when we look at the changing role of the profession, but its central characteristic is very simple. It is a move away from an approach where evaluating the developmental needs of an organization consisted of asking, once a year, which courses a department thought it would need over the next 12 months, towards something much more assertive. It is a shift from the role of passive order taker to proactive business/performance consultant.

This move enables L&D to break out of what David Wilson, MD of European HR Analyst firm Fosway Group, calls the 'conspiracy of convenience' (Jennings, 2010). This conspiracy exists when someone in an organization (usually a manager) asks for training without exploring the root causes of a performance issue, without considering whether this particular course is the right solution to it, and indeed, without considering whether training is the answer at all. The L&D department sources and supplies the training, evaluates the employees' immediate reaction to it, and supplies a summary of the reaction to the original manager. L&D believes it has done its job, as does the manager, and the employees are happy to have received a day out of the office. The problem: there was no clearly defined business driver for the training, and so no way of measuring any impact. Everyone, conveniently, believes they have done their job. In reality nothing has changed.

Very often when this happens the problem is not one that training would ever solve. When a manager calls the training department and asks for a time management course for his or her team, usually training is the last thing the team needs. The team may not be working efficiently, but too often that is not because of a skills or knowledge gap. Usually the issue lies in the employees' working environment, or their motivation, things that training will never fix.

If the L&D department acts as a mere order taker for courses when confronted with a situation like this, and sets up and delivers the training unquestioningly, it does a disservice to the employees, to the manager, to the organization and to its own reputation. The time management course, or the sales day, or the diversity training, is very unlikely to make a difference. Learning will continue to be seen as a reward or punishment for employees, rather than as a key method for changing behaviour and improving performance.

To prevent this happening, L&D can assess requests for training using the discipline of performance consulting.

The importance of trust

The idea of performance consulting for L&D has been with us since at least 1995, the year that Dana Gaines and James C Robinson published *Performance Consulting: Moving beyond training*. My copy of that edition sits on my desk as I write this, with the front cover carrying this quote from William Byham, CEO of DDI Inc: 'The world is changing, and HRD [Human Resource Development] must change with it. Every HRD and training professional who wants to have a job past the year 2000 should read this book.' (Robinson and Robinson, 1995)

Byham was right about our transforming world, and about the importance of performance consulting. He may have been slightly optimistic about how quickly L&D would change. Twenty years after the book was published, performance consulting is only now becoming established as a crucial discipline for the Learning and Development profession.

It is a crucial tool because – as noted previously – the way we use information at work is changing, and is increasingly important to the success of organizations. At the same time, traditional methods of training with scheduled courses are no longer sufficient to meet organizational learning needs. Performance consulting provides a method for finding the causes that lie beneath the symptoms of subpar performance.

One prominent proponent of performance consulting is Nigel Harrison. The author of three useful books on the topic, Nigel is a chartered business psychologist as well as a former e-learning entrepreneur. He and his team of associates work with a growing international client base to help L&D professionals become performance consultants. For anyone involved in L&D I would recommend: *How to be a True Business Partner* (2008) and *How to Deal with Power and Manipulation* (2014), both published by Performance Consulting UK Ltd, and *Improving Employee Performance* (Kogan Page, 2000).

Nigel has a seven-stage process for performance consulting, which he groups into three stages (Harrison, 2008):

1 Building trust and rapport.

2 Facing up to the problem.

3 Building powerful solutions.

L&D too often jumps in at stage 3 – suggesting an answer to the problem straight away without any exploration of the detail of the issue. Nigel calls this 'solutioneering', and it is a common issue in many professions where people know a lot about their subject and want to repeat what seemed to work last time they faced a similar problem.

Solutioneering, like the conspiracy of convenience, seldom works, because it starts with the answer, rather than beginning with a real exploration of the issue at hand. And before that exploration (Nigel's stage 2), it is crucial to establish trust. The importance of trust at the beginning of the relationship between learning technology implementer and client is echoed by those who have succeeded in some of the most difficult of learning technology implementations.

During a stint as an LMS implementation specialist with Domino's Pizza Group in London in 2016, Dionne Hamilton Smith took the somewhat unusual step of driving to see franchisees in person before beginning implementing their instance of the corporate LMS. Her reasoning: 'They were franchisees. I didn't have the authority to tell anyone to do anything. The thing I had to build in the first place was trust. Without that, we knew the implementation would fail.' She was right. Each franchisee owner runs their own business. They are highly successful, hard-driven and focused entirely on results. They will not engage with any initiative that does not help them achieve their goals. Dionne's approach was straightforward. 'I would sit in front of them and listen. The key was understanding what made it tick for them. Then, once I had that, I could respond saying, "Okay, that's your issue. We can help."'

This emphasis on trust is not uncommon in business psychology, but it is not usually given any prominence in discussions about implementing learning technologies. It is, however, vital for success, because when an implementation hits rough going you need people to pull for you, to provide help and use their influence on behalf of you and your project. It is too late to begin building trust when you hit the problem, or indeed at any point during the implementation. The latest trust building should begin is at the very beginning of the implementation. It should really start well before.

Very often, it seems, the business of building trust and rapport with the organization is done inadvertently by people who have had time to learn their way around the organization and build a powerful network. That takes time, but many successful implementations are carried out by people who have indeed been at their company for a number of years – Megan Garrett had been with Hershey's 16 years at the time her implementation began.

Serving time alone is not enough to build trust, though. What matters is how you use that time. A track record of solidly doing the day job well goes a long way towards building it. An L&D department that is professional and delivers on time is halfway there. That professionalism includes making sure that the bread-and-butter work of onboarding and compliance – the bane of many L&D departments' lives – is neatly and efficiently taken care of. It also helps to have engaged a range of people in the business in conversations about what concerns them – professionally and perhaps personally – and not about L&D. These conversations are a great way of establishing common ground that makes any subsequent conversation easier to start and smoother to run. Such conversations need not be very long, and can be quite impromptu – if managed right. When she was head of IT training at the UK Houses of Parliament, Denise Hudson Lawson had a smart use for the muffins left over after a day's training. She would take them through the offices, distributing them on people's desks and stopping for a short chat – a perfect way to build a network and spread goodwill at the same time.

Much of the rest of trust building comes when discussing an actual performance problem. Your accumulated social capital, built on years of doing your job well and engaging professionally with the rest of the business, gets you off to a good start, but once in the conversation about an actual performance problem other things come into play – most notably, the way you conduct the conversation will largely influence perception of you.

Uncovering what is valuable

In these conversations it is vital to present yourself as a professional consultant with a deal of useful expertise and knowledge, but also as someone ready to listen. There are many detailed ways in which to convey this impression – for example, sit next to the person like a colleague, rather than opposite them like an order taker. Mirror their body language, and when speaking absolutely avoid the crime of 'solutioneering'. But in order to really uncover where the performance issue is, and how the person you are talking to would measure its value, the key is to ask the right sort of questions. Your questions should be:

- **Open** – impossible to answer with a single word, so that you invite further elaboration. For example, you might ask 'Who is involved in this?' You could also ask 'Who is affected by this?' a question which also has the benefit of being engaging.

- **Engaging** – inviting the other person to engage their senses and their emotions. For example, rather than asking 'What is the cost of this performance problem?' you might ask 'What will happen if things continue like this?' To get the other person emotionally invested in the problem, you could ask 'What does it look/feel like to do this?' – and use the same question, or a variant, to establish what a better situation might look like.

- **Challenging** – your questions must push the other person into areas they haven't considered as part of the problem. Thinking of the AMO model, if they are focused on the A – Ability, or skills and knowledge, then challenge them to consider the M (Motivation) and O (Opportunity) with questions such as: 'Does it matter to them?' 'Are they rewarded for poor performance?' and 'Do they have all they need for the job?'

This overview only scratches the surface of the detail of how to explore a problem together with an internal client, rather than accept at face value what is presented to you. There are many communications techniques that you can use to really understand the full scope of a problem, and the range of people involved in, and affected, by it.

Dealing with manipulation

While in conversation, it is quite possible that managers will revert to typical buyer–order taker behaviours, treating you as nothing like a trusted consultant. When they do this, they are being manipulative. This may not be deliberate. From conversations with those he has trained in performance consulting, Nigel Harrison reckons that 90 per cent of the time such manipulation is innocent, the reaction of busy managers reverting to type, and just trying to get another issue off their desks. Such a manager, says Nigel, will often state something as a *fait accompli*, using phraseology such as: 'They need sales training. Can you get it organized by June? I have the budget agreed by the exec.'

These 18 words are a masterclass in the shorthand of power politics. They begin with a dual assumption that the person has made. By saying 'They', it is clear the manager has decided on the target audience and 'need sales training' establishes that the required intervention has already been established. 'Can you get it organized' makes it clear that your role is now administrative, the organizer of training rather than a trusted consultant offering useful advice. The kicker comes at the end: 'I have the budget agreed by the exec.' shows that the manager is more powerful than you are, while those two words 'by June' indicate that he or she has already agreed to a timetable that you are now somehow responsible for. That is a lot to pack into 18 words, but people do this all the time (Harrison, 2008).

In sales terms, this would be known as a 'presumptive close'. The manager is closing the conversation with a presumption – several presumptions, in fact, the burden of which is that you are going to do what has been decided elsewhere. In response, it is vital not to slip into the expected role of order taker. Key techniques here involve restating your purpose in the conversation. You might say 'My role as the head of this learning technology implementation is to understand the full scope of the issues here, and all the people affected. As part of that, I'd like to ask a few questions. Can you help me understand the scope in more detail?' In doing this you neither passively accept the implicit order, but neither are you aggressive. Rather, you are acting as a seasoned, professional consultant. Keeping the conversation in that frame – as a discussion between adults – is key to continuing to building trust, and to being taken seriously.

It is difficult for the manager to respond negatively to the question 'Can you help me understand the scope in more detail?' They might say something like 'I don't see what else there is to say.' But in the absence of a flat 'No', you can go on to use the questioning techniques described above as part of a collaborative approach that really gets to the heart of the performance issue, and how it is perceived by the manager.

What we can take from performance consulting, then, is that establishing trust is essential – ideally before any conversations with stakeholders. That trust will get you into the conversation in a good light. The techniques of performance consulting will enable you to get to the root of any performance issue, which can be tackled with a learning technology in a way that both sides agree. From this you will then have an idea what type of implementation you will need – type 1, 2 or 3 (starting at type 4 is probably only in the gift of those at the head of the organization). Because you will know what the value is to the manager you have been talking to, you will also know how to measure its impact – with a hard metric that can be counted, or a softer, less tangible measure.

Establishing the aim of a learning technology implementation is more complex than either asking a manager for the aim, or deciding it independently. It involves some discussion and interplay between executives, managers and L&D professionals, just one instance of the complex interactions with people that make up much of the non-technical side of an implementation, and which we explore in more detail in the next chapter.

Key takeaways

1   Learning technology implementations have four possible, non-exclusive aims – to improve business as usual, to make L&D more efficient, to make learning more effective, or as part of an organizational cultural change programme.

2   Each of these implementation types may have an impact that can be measured by an existing business metric.

3   Each implementation may also have intangible benefits which cannot be easily measured, but which are still of benefit to the organization.

4   At the very beginning of an implementation project, it is crucial to understand what the aim and value of the implementation are, and how (if at all) that value can be measured. Without an aim and a sense of value, it is impossible to keep on track or to know if you have succeeded.

5   While it is possible to run a Return on Investment (ROI) study to see the impact of an implementation, it may not be simple. Consider an impact study instead.

6   ROI is a well-defined term, often misused and abused, and is not a synonym for every post-implementation benefit. Only use the term to refer to a genuine, rigorous ROI study.

7   The AMO model states that performance is a function of Ability, Motivation and Opportunity. Learning and training only affect the first of these three factors.

8   Performance consulting consists of asking open, engaging and challenging questions to get to heart of a performance problem, beneath the superficial symptoms.

9 Performance consulting conversations require the ability to build trust before engaging in dialogue and the political astuteness to tackle manipulation.

10 Performance consulting questioning techniques are a highly effective way of establishing both the aim for a learning technology implementation and the value that it must demonstrate.

References

BBC (2011) [accessed 13 December 2016] Southern Cross set to shut down and stop running homes, 11 July, [Online] http://www.bbc.co.uk/news/business-14102750

Boxall, P and Purcell, J (2002) *Strategy and Human Resource Management*, Palgrave Macmillan, New York

Cavendish (2013) [accessed 13 December 2016] The Cavendish Review: An independent review into healthcare assistants and support workers in the NHS and social care settings, *HM Government*, July, [Online] https://www.gov.uk/government/uploads/system/uploads/attachment_data/file/236212/Cavendish_Review.pdf

CERTPOINT Systems Inc (2012) [accessed 13 December 2016] Showing the impact of learning: How can we demonstrate the impact of learning? [Online] http://www.cedma-europe.org/newsletter%20articles/misc/Impact%20of%20Learning%20Whitepaper%20(Jul%2012).pdf

Economist, The (2008) [accessed 13 December 2016] The Hawthorne Effect, *The Economist*, [Online] http://www.economist.com/node/12510632

Harrison, N (2008) *How to be a True Business Partner by Performance Consulting*, Nigel Harrison, London

Jennings, C (2010) [accessed 13 December 2016] Five Barriers to Effective Learning in Organisations, [Online] http://charles-jennings.blogspot.co.uk/2010/04/five-barriers-to-effective-learning-in.html

Learning Technologies (2012) [accessed 13 December 2016] Learning Technologies Conference 2012 – Matt DeFeo – proving the impact of business-led learning, [Online] https://www.youtube.com/watch?v=YiXiwU9Mo-o

Linthicum, D S (1999) *Enterprise Application Integration*, Third edition, Addison-Wesley, Boston

Moore, G A (1998) *Crossing the Chasm: Marketing and selling technology products to mainstream customers*, Capstone Publishing, Oxford

Rackham, N (1988) *SPIN Selling*, McGraw-Hill, New York

Robinson, D G G and Robinson, J C (1995) *Performance Consulting: Moving beyond training*, Berrett-Koehler, San Francisco

Rogers, E M (2003) *Diffusion of Innovations*, Fifth edition, The Free Press, New York

ROI Institute (2014) [accessed 13 December 2016] The proliferation of learning technologies calls for a method to measure their success, [Online] http://www.roiinstitute.net/wp-content/uploads/2014/12/ROI-Calculations-Article_Dec-14.pdf

Thalheimer, W (2006) [accessed 25 November 2016] Spacing Learning over Time, *Work-Learning Research Inc.*, [Online] http://willthalheimer.typepad.com/files/spacing_learning_over_time_2006.pdf

Towards Maturity (2013) [accessed 13 December 2016] Delivering the Kindest Care at HC-One, [Online] http://www.towardsmaturity.org/elements/uploads/HC-One_case_study.pdf

People focus 10

I was constantly astonished by the extraordinary dreams of ordinary people. STUDS TERKEL, *WORKING*

You can do anything with technology, but people can also stop you doing just about everything. ANDY WOOLER, ACADEMY TECHNOLOGY MANAGER, HITACHI DATA SYSTEMS

In his 1972 book *Working*, Studs Terkel, that extraordinary chronicler of oral history, lays out hundreds of interviews with working Americans, who reveal the hopes, frustrations and realities of their daily lives. Like all of Terkel's books of interviews, it is a vivid insight into how other people think, an invitation to step outside our own ways of seeing the world – in this book, the world of work – and take on another viewpoint. It took Terkel three years to write the book: researching, interviewing, transcribing and finding what he calls the 'gold' in each person's story.

When implementing a learning technology, it would be wonderful to have the amount of time that Terkel had to explore what the people in an organization want and need. It would also be wonderful to have his gift of both asking the right questions and listening so well that people laid bare their thoughts and feelings in response. We will never have as much time as we would like to explore the context of an implementation, but when we do speak, we must always aim to ask the right questions and to listen well to what people say in response. It is only by being aware of what people think, and feel, about their work and the learning technology we will make available to them, that we can make a success of it. Terkel was right. People do have extraordinary dreams. Good L&D can help them to fulfil those dreams, at every level of the organization. The alternative, too often, is that L&D is seen as a chore, as something to be avoided if possible. Andy Wooler alludes to when he says: 'People can also stop you doing just about everything.' When people don't care about a project, when they cannot see a good reason for it, it will not succeed.

This chapter is about the second part of the APPA approach – the focus on people. This focus has to take in *all* the people involved in making the implementation a success, as well as those affected by it. This is a wide set of people, starting with the people who will use the technology, but including managers, vendors, those on the implementation team and others. In the course of this chapter we will look at four key parts of focusing on people: understanding who they are; communicating with them effectively; being aware of their different perspectives when launching a learning technology; and finally, working with them to sustain the technology post-launch.

People at the heart of an implementation

Herman Miller is a manufacturer of contemporary interior furnishings, solutions for the healthcare environment, and related technologies and services headquartered in Zeeland, Michigan. Now employing about 8,000 people worldwide, the company was originally founded in 1905. From that bald description, Herman Miller might seem an unlikely home for innovation. Yet, although it has been inducted into the Made in USA Hall of Fame for its commitment to US Manufacturing, and been celebrated for the quality of its sales, supply and – especially – for its design, there is another side to the company. It has received numerous awards for sustainability, commitment to diversity, corporate equality and trustworthiness. This manufacturer clearly knows the value of its employees.

This people focus was reflected in 2013, when the company rolled out an Electronic Performance Support System (EPSS) for its sales team of 800 internationally. The EPSS was to support the introduction of a new, cloud-based Customer Relationship Management system (CRM). Implementing two systems at once is no inconsiderable feat, but only part of a considerable change challenge the company had set itself. The new CRM was the main driver in introducing a fresh approach to selling, which introduced extensive procedural changes. In its turn, the EPSS introduced an entirely new way of learning – learning what is required at the point of need, rather than the traditional approach of trying to learn everything at the start of the implementation, via face-to-face training. This shift to a performance-focused mode of learning was based on the thinking of Bob Mosher and Conrad Gottfredson, and their five points of learning need, which we saw in Chapter 2. Moving to this approach often involves a substantial shift in the way people think about learning, asking them to abandon the schoolroom assumption and take much greater personal responsibility for their learning.

Building the team right

Altogether the change programme involved a considerable amount of both technical and cultural complexity. Jeremy Smith, Senior Manager Global Learning Solutions for Herman Miller, was in charge of the learning component. Managing this part alone involved a team of 22, including sales executives, IT executives, supply management, marketing, IT implementation experts, sales process subject matter experts, a dedicated team (design, development, project management) from the supplier, a cross-functional change management team and a cross-functional project management team. Jeremy represented this EPSS implementation team on the CRM launch core team, which involved the most senior leaders.

Not all of the 22 involved in implementing the EPSS worked on the project full time, but even so, for a target group of 800 users, this was a large number, certainly large enough to risk creating more problems than it solved. From previous implementations of LMSs and other systems, Jeremy was aware this could be problematic and from the start intentionally set out to mitigate any issues. He put in place operating agreements to ensure responsibilities and communications lines were clear, so that it was possible to escalate problems to a higher managerial level if necessary.

The operating agreements were there to deal with things when communications broke down. As Jeremy puts it, they answered some tough questions: 'How are we going to treat each other when we have a concern about something? How do you speak up in the room? We set a mechanism in place upfront for dealing with all this.' This process of explicitly accepting that communications between people could break down had an unexpected consequence – individuals' teamworking competency actually increased over the course of the project, because the operating agreements provided an objective, external, view of what effective behaviour looked like. By preparing for possible breakdowns in interpersonal relations, team members thought consciously about how to deal with each other, and adjusting their behaviour, rather than waiting until something went wrong, and hoping they could deal with it.

In many ways, the complex team structure demanded by the project was not ideal, says Jeremy, but there was no alternative, any more than there was an alternative to a considerable amount of planning required. He realized this when he worked back from the final requirement: an international team of 800 field sales people had to become competent on a new CRM system, complete with new sales processes and behaviours, with no break in sales effort. From his background in implementing other systems, and in live instruction, Jeremy knew the traditional approach would not work: a training needs analysis, followed by definitions of learning objectives, which would in turn have led to hours, possibly days, of virtual and physical classroom training on the CRM, a traditional 'big bang' launch of the system and then a frantic period on the helpdesks until things settled down. 'I reverse engineered it. I saw how the introduction of the CRM system was putting pressure not just on the learning organization, but on the IT organization and the end users themselves.'

From knowing that a traditional training approach would not help sales people use the CRM effectively, Jeremy worked back to finding a different solution, and ended up with the idea of providing performance support to the sales team during the CRM implementation, rather than trying to fill their heads with every possible piece of knowledge beforehand.

In the end, this move from Instructor-Led Training (ILT) to performance support was enthusiastically embraced by others in the company. They saw not only a learning solution that worked, but also a new way of working with the Learning and Development department. Jeremy puts it this way: 'For better or worse, I've been meeting with a lot of the same clients for many, many years doing organizational change and technology change, and so they noticed that we were having a very different conversation, and it felt different and more productive and more meaningful to them.'

The pitch

While the solution and approach may have been enthusiastically embraced at the end of the process, how did Jeremy convince the organizational leadership in the first place that changing from ILT to performance support was a good idea? Initially, he says, he talked to a range of 'executives, sponsors, stakeholders, sales leaders, end users and implementers' to determine what mattered most to them, and then made his pitch. Given the scope of the project – the number of people, their geographical distribution, and the amount they had to learn – there was a strong case for using an EPSS to support the new CRM system on the basis of the resource implications alone. Live training would have been prohibitively expensive. That would have made his pitch a straightforward type 2 solution: doing the old things in a more efficient way. In addition, though, Jeremy was explicit about the need for a different way of learning. The aim was to provide 'an effective moment-of-need approach to learning that could be used for both launch/onboarding, and over time, while minimizing disruption to the selling process'. This would make this a type 3 implementation, where learning takes place in a new way. Beyond that, however, Jeremy was aware of the need to support a larger aim. As he puts it 'It was not realistic to think that a big splash of formal learning could achieve the significant and sustained change required by sales leadership'. In other words, this was explicitly a learning programme supporting organizational change. It was a type 4 implementation with strong supporting arguments based on efficiency and effectiveness.

When a pitch is in sync with a corporate change initiative, can make learning both more effective and efficient and is expressed in language that resonates with stakeholders, it should certainly succeed, and Jeremy's did.

Responsiveness through agility

Having won the pitch, the team was ready to begin needs analysis and development of the learning platform, using an Agile design approach. 'Agile helped keep the needs analysis and design phases objective and focused on critical performance,' says Jeremy, 'on what learners needed to do rather than what they needed to know. This approach was also selected because of the ability to use it over time as the CRM evolved and new performance needs emerged. A version of the original job task and critical skills analysis tool is still in use today.'

The influential *Manifesto for Agile Software Development* was published in 2001, and is an approach to software development based on 12 principles. While accepting the necessity of planning, it places great emphasis on communication and rapid iterations of software and frequent testing for the generation of feedback. Among the principles are (Agile Alliance, 2015):

1 Our highest priority is to satisfy the customer through early and continuous delivery of valuable software.

2 Welcome changing requirements, even late in development. Agile processes harness change for the customer's competitive advantage.

4 Business people and developers must work together daily through-out the project.

6 The most efficient and effective method of conveying infor-mation to and within a development team is face-to-face conversation.

12 At regular intervals, the team reflects on how to become more effective, then tunes and adjusts its behavior accordingly.

Although the principles relate to software development, some at least are clearly very relevant for L&D systems implementations. As we have already seen, the team emphasized self-awareness and developing the process of teamwork (principle 12) using operating agreements. The other principles came into play as the teams specified the product, prototyped and tested it.

Listening during the pilot

For Jeremy's team, piloting the EPSS was certainly about testing the technology, but that was just a basic requirement. More than that, they wanted a sense of everything around the use of the system: was it intuitive enough? Was authentication working as expected? 'We were quite intentional about piloting the entire change management process. I think learning technologies sometimes set themselves up for difficulty when they focus solely on piloting the tool.' According to Jeremy they wanted users to be clear 'why and when they'd use it, that their managers understood why and when they'd use it, that we were giving them clear and concise instructions around both those things.' In piloting the platform, then, they tested everything from the first, introductory e-mail, all the way through to gathering and reporting analytics back to the business leaders.

The pilot with a representative group of about 40 sales people and managers generated exactly the sort of practical feedback they were looking for on functional and content adaptations to the tool. It also, however, made them realize something rather more fundamental: the sales employees were unclear as to the exact role of the tool. It was neither a helpdesk online, nor a course. 'We realized that if we were going to call this performance support, we actually need to take time to educate the end user on that concept.' To do this, they used Mosher and Gottfredson's five moments of needs as a simple way to help people understand what performance support is. Following the pilot, his team adapted the messaging to describe performance support and help users identify for themselves when they had a particular learning need, and understand the best way of meeting it, whether by using the system, or – if it really was the best option – by calling the support desk.

The pilot also tested management reporting – presenting activity measures to a group of about 80 sales leaders to gauge their reaction. These sales leaders were charged with driving the CRM implementation, and the learning team with providing data to show how the EPSS was being used in each region. The initial reaction to the reporting was not positive. Like the sales teams, the managers were unfamiliar with the idea of performance support. When the first group saw thousands of very short transactions, their initial interpretation was that their sales people were entering the system and leaving virtually immediately. Their conclusion: the EPSS was a complete failure. It was up to the learning team to recast their interpretation of the data as a success, to show that short transactions meant people had found the support they were looking for and were getting back to work quickly. Following that feedback from the first group of managers, Jeremy's team realized the value of adding an extra layer of reporting, showing the number of pages visited, and the pathways of people entering and exiting the tool, demonstrating the value of the EPSS. This focus on people and their reactions, working with them, continued into the launch phase and beyond.

Focus groups for feedback

The EPSS and CRM were phased in by region, with about 100 people a week adopting the system over the course of eight weeks. The schedule was driven by the IT department wanting to scale at the right pace, allowing it to deal with any issues one by one, rather than all at once. Jeremy's team took a similarly scaled approach, revealing the functionality of the EPSS in stages. The system contained 150 'support objects', or pieces of content. Rather than overload users with all of these at once, the learning team revealed just 15 support objects, at first, covering the survival skills for the new system. A week later that was doubled to 30 objects, until by week four, they had access to the whole set of content. Managing this gradual reveal of content within the staged roll out was a complex task, but it was appreciated by the system users. They wanted to focus on selling, not on learning how to use an entirely new CRM system.

In any technical implementation, knowing users' reaction is crucial – to judge how far you are meeting the project aims. Gathering frequent feedback is also very much in line with the principles of the Agile approach, along with welcoming changing requirements. If done properly, a real focus on people and true communication with them will inevitably result in tweaks and changes, as the planned implementation bumps up against the reality of usage. What is the best way of gathering this feedback?

Principle 6 of the Agile Manifesto says 'The most efficient and effective method of conveying information… is face-to-face conversation', but this was impossible with such a dispersed team of sales people. Instead, the team used online meeting software to run live focus groups online. In running these, the team adhered to some tight guidelines to ensure a trusting environment and plenty of useful vocal interaction and feedback:

1 No more than 12 people per group – to encourage dialogue.

2 Enough time spent on personal introductions to build trust.

3 The same question set for all groups – to ensure consistent data.

4 A limited question set – to allow for conversation and exploration.

5 A group facilitator and a note taker – to allow each to focus on their task.

6 Recording everything – so nothing was missed.

7 A set duration, religiously adhered to.

8 A wide, representative sample of users.

The EPSS team set the duration of their meetings at 60 minutes, allowing enough time to discuss the six agreed questions in depth. When the idea of focus groups was first raised, the project team wanted to ask dozens of questions, according to Jeremy, exploring user reaction to a wide range of functionality. In the end, however, the team agreed that a smaller number of open questions that stimulated conversation was preferable to a lot of simple checks on functionality. Dealing with the responses and drawing out opinion took a skilled facilitator, especially given that there was no video used, and the facilitator could only hear the participants' voices. That is why it was essential to allow the facilitator to concentrate entirely on that role and have a different team member take notes.

Quite deliberately, the team did not try to include everyone in the focus groups. Instead, they collected enough feedback to represent the whole. After all, the explicit aim was to support and improve the sales process, not to interrupt it. They ran three focus groups to cover the entire pilot cohort of about 40, because that feedback was essential to guide the subsequent implementation. Then, during the roll out proper, they ran two focus groups with sales leaders, covering about a quarter of these managers in total. The thinking was that the sales leaders would have valuable feedback on how their team members were using the system, as well as a wider insight from a managerial viewpoint. Finally, they ran two open forums, so that anyone who felt strongly about giving feedback had an opportunity.

Many learning technology implementations drive towards a launch, or finish line, but as Jeremy puts it, with cloud-based software regularly updated by the vendor, 'there really is no finish line' for a performance support system. Even after launch, the content needs regular revision. This means that, long after the actual roll out, Jeremy continues to actively cultivate the relationships set up during the implementation.

Sustained vendor relationships

Among those he keeps in contact with are the two vendors that began the entire process. If this implementation was a success it was because Jeremy established not only strong relations with them individually, but also cultivated a positive working relationship between them.

With many years' experience of implementations, Jeremy knew that the worst position for the L&D team was to be in the middle of two or more vendors, shuffling information between them. It was simply, in his words 'terribly inefficient' to relay very technical data about matters such as single sign on, and the inner workings of a cloud-based EPSS. In this particular implementation, user authentication was complex and potentially a barrier to finishing the project on time. The answer: have the vendors talk to each other, in detail and openly, to solve issues as they arose. Vendors are typically reticent about doing this, and each for different reasons. Some jealously guard their intellectual property. Others want to retain an individual relationship with the client. Jeremy's approach is to 'get to the source of their reluctance'. Using the sort of open questioning and listening we explored earlier under performance consulting, Jeremy was able to find ways of ensuring variously that intellectual property was protected and that the relationship between Herman Miller and the vendor remained strong.

Once the 'source of reluctance' was found for each vendor, Jeremy's next step was to create what he calls 'a new context' for them. That context is that they were working together, on a team, for Herman Miller, with all the long-term commitment that implies. Establishing this context took time and energy, but immeasurably improved the speed and quality of communication during the implementation and afterwards. Two years after the initial relationships with vendors were established, and well after the platform was launched, an anomaly occurred. A small group of users was unable to authenticate. Having established a strong relationship in the first place, and kept it open, Jeremy was able to raise the issue with the vendors' technical experts and the internal IT team without the need to either seek permission or build a new relationship. As Jeremy puts it, those relationships have become increasingly important not least for reasons of speed. 'In a cloud-based world, you can come in one day and it won't be working because someone's changed something... it's crucial to form these relationships and keep them active.'

I have told the story of the Herman Miller implementation at length because it illustrates in real-world terms how a focus on people, and communicating well with them, is not an adjunct to a learning technologies implementation, but an essential part of it.

Key groups

If people are core to a learning technologies implementation, it is essential to know who they are. Here's a short run down of the key stakeholders to consider.

Your team

Your team could range from one person to a considerable number, and might be full time, part time, or a combination of the two. If the core team is larger than about eight, consider using explicit terms of reference, and operating agreements such as Jeremy deployed. It will make people conscious of the need to think about how they interact, and to do it well.

It may be that the implementation will alter the roles of some people in the L&D department. If this looks likely – as it did with Hershey's content producers – then make it a priority to get these people on board and enthusiastic early on.

The IT department

It is striking how often the people involved in successful learning technologies implementations have an existing relationship with their IT department, as with Jeremy Smith, who had spent years working with IT at Herman Miller. Nobody responds well to attempts to build a relationship – personal or professional – with a request for help or to discuss the things that are important to the other party. Your IT department is no exception. It is far better to have invested the time in building the relationship in advance, to have helped each other out in the small ways that create a binding relationship.

There is a tendency to believe that the IT department is less important as software moves to the cloud because applications are not hosted on site. While the department may be less involved with local software administration, it still controls the IT environment of the workplace, sets the IT policy and has to be involved in decision-making that affects employees. Herman Miller's CRM and the EPSS supporting it were both cloud-based.

Executives and managers

Executives (those at the upper echelons of a company) and managers (those closer to daily operations) are crucial to the success of any implementation. Executives will typically sign off a pitch, while managers are crucial to the project's success; it is they, after all, who determine how employees spend their time. It is fashionable today to underplay the role of managers, but anyone wondering about their impact on organizational effectiveness should read the 2012 *Harvard Business Review* paper 'Does Management Really Work?' The short answer: companies in the top third of management practice are 23 per cent more productive than those in the bottom third (Bloom *et al*, 2012).

Partners and vendors

Any reasonably sized implementation will involve vendors and/
or partners. An enterprise LMS implementation – on-site or on the
cloud – is likely to go more smoothly with an implementation partner. We saw above how important it was to build strong relationships
with – and between – the vendors during the Herman Miller implementation, and to sustain them afterwards.

Those using the system

If you don't engage with those using the learning technology you
are implementing, there is no point starting work, because you
will fail. 'Engage' does not, of course, mean 'tell them what's going
to happen'. It means 'talk and listen'. Consider the rapid product
development approach mentioned in Chapter 7, constantly seeking
feedback and frequently iterating the product to test and improve
it. That is real engagement, as was the use Jeremy Smith's team
made of focus groups, and their agile response to the feedback they
received. In a large, dispersed implementation, it is worth considering a group of 'super users' who can be early adopters of the system,
give support to those around them, and provide feedback from
themselves and from co-workers from pilot stage through to maintenance. This real-world input can be vital to successful adoption of
the technology.

This list of five key groups is by no means exhaustive. There will be
others in your own environment. Whoever they are, your stakeholders need to be sought out and listened to, for they are where your
project will thrive or fail.

Stakeholder analysis

Stakeholder analysis is a way of targeting key influencers to ensure
the success of a project. There are many different approaches to
stakeholder analysis, but across them all the following steps are
consistent:

1 Identify your stakeholders.

2 List their interests and expectations regarding the project and their influence on it.

3 Determine their enthusiasm for, and impact on, the project.

4 Plan your actions to maintain or (if necessary) increase their enthusiasm.

Identifying your stakeholders is often best done by brainstorming a list with the rest of your team. The list could include any of the key groups above as well as groups you have identified yourself, and some key individuals.

In step 2, when listing your stakeholders' interests and expectations, you may need to divide some of the groups up. Not all employees are the same, nor all managers. The stakeholders' expectations should be drawn upon from real interviews, not based on guesswork or assumption. During these interviews it is crucial to use open questions and to listen carefully for nuanced, political answers that might need further exploration. For an EPSS supporting the roll out of a major booking system in a hotel chain, the list might look like this (Table 10.1).

The 'priority' column here can be as simple as this three-point scale, or be more granular. The *Harvard Business Review* guide to stakeholder analysis suggests using five points (Applegate, 2008).

The table can also include more detail. Tiffany Prince, of Chicago-based Prince Performance LLC, specializes in project managing complex learning technologies implementations. Her stakeholder analysis matrix has no fewer than eight columns:

- Target stakeholder
- Change to current activity
- New behaviour
- Concerns
- Sources of resistance
- What's a win?
- Who takes action?
- Action

Table 10.1 Stakeholder interests and expectations

Stakeholder	Priority	Perceived value and outlook
Sales manager, North	High	Looking for sales processing to continue uninterrupted. Sceptical – sees new booking system as interruption to business as usual.
Operations director	High	Main executive sponsor, won't budge on tight deadlines, but will provide support. Pet project, so keen to be associated with success.
Booking team, North	High	Under pressure to deliver uninterrupted service from manager. High turnover of staff. Looking for support.
Sales team leader, East	Medium	Sales team established and tech savvy. Confident they will handle roll out with EPSS support. Will make displeasure clear if they don't.
IT manager	Medium	Established contact, on implementation team. Would prefer staged roll out, but accepts this is impossible.
Reception team, South	Low	Should not be heavily impacted, provided sales team fully trained. Team and manager positive.
... etc		

Putting all this information on one sheet has the advantage of providing a clear set of guidelines for the questions you might ask during interview, and acts as a guide for the action to take as a result.

In the third step of this process, determining the stakeholders' enthusiasm for, and impact on, the project is usually done by plotting them on a grid like Figure 10.1.

This grid provides a good tool for stimulating and refining conversation among implementation team members – the discussion while placing the stakeholders on the grid can throw up more detail about what is driving the particular stakeholder, and resolve ambiguities about what is driving a person or group. Once they are placed on the grid, the action to take with each participant is clarified (Figure 10.2).

Figure 10.1   The Stakeholder Analysis Grid

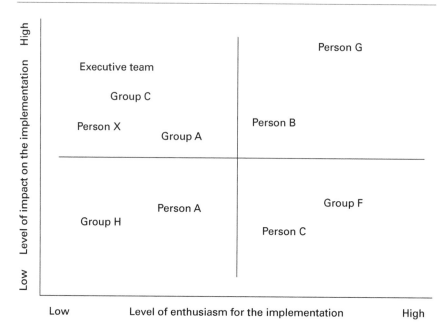

Figure 10.2   Actions on the Stakeholder Analysis Grid

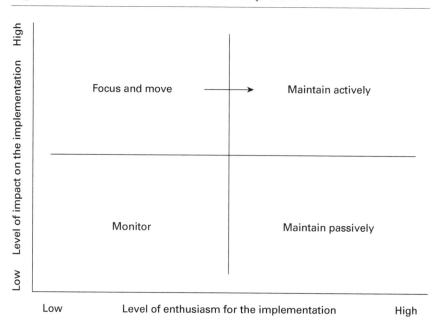

The greatest priority is to move those with a high potential impact from a negative to a positive view of the implementation, or at least to a neutral position. Hence the need to 'focus and move' them to the top-right quadrant. If it is not possible to make them feel entirely positively about the project, it is important to open and maintain lines of communication so you can pick up on any negative reaction immediately and react to it. Like Don Corleone in *The Godfather*, you should insist on being a man or woman 'who insists on hearing bad news immediately'.

The same applies to those who are negative about the implementation but unable to influence it. It is crucial to keep them in touch with the positive effects of the implementation, and to monitor their reactions. However, it is not necessary actively to attempt to change their feelings about the implementation. It may be an impossible task and that energy would be better spent elsewhere.

Those who are already positive about the implementation need to be kept that way. If they can influence it, then actively engage them via communication and by soliciting feedback. If not, then keep a watching brief only. Inform them about the value of the implementation, and give them a way of feeding back useful input and thoughts, but do not spend time actively seeking these out. It is very tempting to spend a lot of time down in the bottom-right quadrant, listening to the opinions of those who think the implementation team are doing a good job. That time would be better spent seeking out their opinion of how the system could be improved.

Once you know who the stakeholders are, the next step is to take action, and to plan communication with them.

Communication

The word 'communicate' has a tendency to be awfully ill-used. I spent about two hours interviewing Jeremy Smith about his implementation for Herman Miller, and in addition he kindly filled out an extensive questionnaire I had provided. In both the interview and the questionnaire, he mentioned stakeholders frequently and explicitly talked about conducting stakeholder analysis. It was also noticeable that he used the words 'communicate' and 'listen' a great deal. One word he hardly used at all was 'e-mail'.

And yet, for too many people 'communicate' is synonymous with the idea of pushing out an idea, and that in turn is synonymous with sending out an e-mail. Of course, Jeremy did use e-mail when piloting the programme, because new users of the EPSS would be informed of the tool via e-mail and he wanted to test how that would work. However, his team invited reaction to these e-mails, and used them to gather useful feedback that led them to change not only how they composed their mails, but also caused them to create a new line of communication, explaining what the performance support system was, and when to use it. In other words, this was e-mail used to communicate, rather than to tell. It was part of a conversation, where listening to the response was important.

Planning your communications

Keeping up a regular stream of communication and listening is crucial to the implementation, from initial pitch to pilot to implementation and maintenance. Megan kept communication open with a wide range of groups at Hershey's, including her HR Business Forum, the LMS Steering Committee and, of course, her own widely dispersed L&D team. Communication with each of these groups was planned, just as Jeremy planned out communication with his stakeholders.

As with stakeholder analysis, there is no set shape of a communications plan, although any communications plan should include the information in the plan below (Table 10.2), set up for our fictional hotel chain implementing an EPSS to support its booking system.

There is no limit to the methods that can be used for communicating. Possibilities include: departmental meetings, webinars, posters, company intranet messages, lunchtime meetings, podcasts, videos, newsletters, internal social media as well as focus groups and, of course, e-mail, if it is used to communicate rather than just to push out information. This stress on two-way communication is conveyed in the detail of not only what the message is, but also what to listen for:

Table 10.2 A communications plan

Stakeholder	Frequency and method	Message/listen for	Assigned to
Sales manager, North	Bi-weekly phone call and regular mail	Message: new system helps sales processing happen faster and is not interrupting work	JB
		Listen for: signs system is not working properly/not being used properly	
Operations director	Weekly personal meeting with team leader, implementation	Message: activity and impact reports, exception reports and narrative of progress to date	TL
		Listen for: concerns on timing, suggestions and contacts	
Central bookings team	Weekly push of new functionality, teaser animation	Message: awareness of latest functionality	TP and DT
		Listen for: e-mails from users, increased support calls, unexpected usage paths through EPSS	
... etc			

The communications plan can be far more comprehensive than this. Learning programme implementation specialist Tiffany Prince suggests it should have 10 columns:

- Date
- Frequency
- Type
- Audience
- Message/Objective
- Method
- Key contact
- Reviewer/Approver
- Action
- Status

Communication before specification

Although it is seldom said explicitly, 'communication' is usually tacitly understood to be synonymous with 'deciding on a message and pushing it out'. So far in this chapter, I have tried to suggest this is a poor definition by stressing the need for communication to be two-way, to include listening. One organization that did this throughout its learning technology implementation was HC-One, the healthcare company mentioned in Chapter 9, which made communication an integral part of its shift towards a culture of high-quality care.

When a company focuses on culture change like this, communications play a major part in establishing the new culture and reinforcing it over time. The company used an extensive, high-quality communications programme to promote its *touch* training programme, and it also listened throughout, even when specifying the programme. The company established a working party of 20 stakeholders in different roles and at different levels within the company. Their input was crucial in guiding the development of the project, just as pilot group feedback was to Jeremy's development of the EPSS programme at Herman Miller. The difference here was that the input came earlier in the process.

The HC-One working party resulted in three key principles to guide the development of the programme, as well as input on how those principles could be put to use. The first principle was to move away from training purely for compliance and instead create a culture of training for quality and kindness. This meant altering the perception that what happened in the classroom was different from what you did when you were back in the real world. The HC-One team called this 'building competent compliance'. One practical implication was to ensure that learning materials made explicit the links between what was learned – for example, the importance of thorough hand washing – to the impact on individual residents who the employees cared about.

The second principle was to embed the learning at work, rather than to create training that belonged in a separate place. This meant providing most of the training via e-learning, and had the practical implication of the need to buy new computers for many care centres.

It also made it essential that the materials were mobile-friendly. Together, these changes were a boon in a working environment dominated by shift work. Those on the night shift were finally able to reach the same quality of materials as their colleagues without having to juggle their domestic and working diaries to attend daytime training.

The third principle was to move the training experience beyond the single event, providing materials with a lasting, ongoing effect. This meant, for example, both providing a video library of materials, such as films of experienced staff members exploring particular topics in depth, as well as very short videos that put over simple key messages in a memorable way – for example, having Sherlock Holmes investigate pressure sores. These short videos served as vivid, sometimes humorous, reminders of important topics. This approach also included the conversation cards for managers, which helped them prompt and steer conversations with colleagues to explore particular issues together. These principles, and their practical implications, came about as a result of actively listening to the suggestions of the working party (LearningTechUK, 2014).

Communication up to launch and beyond

As well as providing input into the design of the programme itself, the HC-One working party helped with suggestions for the communications plan promoting it. This plan began well before the system launch date and continued throughout the project, using different media to contact different stakeholders in the way that was best for them.

The first communications were reports to the board. Next came the task of working with the company's learning facilitators, to explain the new approach early on, and to understand their reaction and tackle any concerns. These people were the face and voice of training internally. If they were behind the programme, it would succeed. Without them, it could not.

The programme included a wide range of media – posters, a roadshow, competitions, and a welcome movie, all elements of a sophisticated communications plan. A less usual, but very effective part of the plan was the selection and training of 'touch ambassadors'. These were, effectively, 'super users', employees trained to support colleagues on how to use the training materials, but also – crucially – on why they should be used. In other words, their role was not purely technical, they conveyed the message of how this approach to learning would improve the professional practice of a particular colleague, and linked it to the welfare of residents.

Finally, post launch, the communications plan continued. Here the focus changed from building up communications prior to launch to maintenance of the message. The short movies continued, along with other content that helped promote the *touch* message. In addition, however, it was now possible to add another line to the communications plan – celebrating success.

Think about the stakeholder grid, with its four quadrants. The success of an implementation post-launch is dependent on keeping the positive people positive and helping shift everyone else a little further to the right on that grid. Although this was a type 4 implementation, focused on a cultural change that was by definition difficult to measure, HC-One was able to point early on to high approval ratings from colleagues using the system, and then later to survey results and managerial reaction, all pointing towards the success of the programme. The success of the *touch* programme was sustained by conveying this information to the stakeholders in the right way for them – whether in a dry fact-focused report, or in a video of a colleague sharing their experiences.

The *touch* programme was a substantial undertaking, tightly integrated with its communications strategy. It is little wonder that HC-One viewed the communications piece of the implementation as a project in its own right, and a crucial element in its success (LearningTechUK, 2014).

The launch

This chapter is all about focusing on people, and how listening to them carefully is an essential part of the success of an implementation. That is not always easy. When interviewing people for this book and looking back over past Learning Technologies Conference presentations, I have always been impressed by those with the courage to seek out the difficult conversations they can learn from, rather than locking themselves away in the training department, or talking only to supporters of their project. I am sure that the HC-One working party and Herman Miller's open focus groups threw up some observations that were tough to take, but invaluable in improving the project.

It has been suggested to me that, however important listening may be, there is one point during an implementation when it becomes redundant: when launching the system. From this point of view, the listening has all taken place in honing the learning technology prior to launch, and it is crucial then to present it to employees as a finished product. Suggesting that it is open to change at this stage is to suggest weakness and to invite a catalogue of change requests that cannot all be fulfilled. It raises expectations only to disappoint at least some of them. Although I can see some value in this view, I do not agree with it. There is always scope, I would suggest, for maintaining two-way communication with the people using a learning technology. Rather than disappointing expectations, we should set the tone of conversation correctly in the first place to prevent that happening.

There are several ways of launching a learning technology, each suited to different circumstances. In each of them there is ample scope for gathering feedback and taking action on it.

The 'big bang' launch

When HC-One launched its *touch* programme, it did so with a 'big bang' launch, announced to the company as a whole by messages across a range of channels. For an initiative that affects everyone in the company, is driven from the top of the organization and which needs the full support of all employees, a big bang approach is the right choice. A well-managed event will create momentum and can be the impetus pushing a change programme towards success.

It remains, however, a high-risk strategy. Nay-sayers will seize on any apparent glitches or errors as evidence of the technology's weakness. The best way to counteract this is to have carried out a full stakeholder analysis in advance. This allows you to be aware of any concerns, to address the ones you can, and to explain what you can or cannot do about the rest. At launch, have watertight technology and feedback mechanisms for everyone involved – for example, if using e-learning hosted on the web, have e-mail addresses, feedback mechanisms and internal social media links on every page used. This will enable you to deal with complaints and valuable suggestions alike, but it will not create all the feedback you need. The richest feedback, and politically the most potentially troublesome, will come as a result of deliberately seeking out difficult conversations with those ill-disposed towards the project. Some of what they say will be useful input. Some of it will be misconceptions you can put right, and some could undermine your implementation if repeated. That's tough to listen to, but worth hearing, and necessary to counteract.

The soft launch

A soft launch lacks the fireworks and pizazz of a big bang launch. Also called a 'staggered' or 'rolling' launch, it consists of releasing the technology to groups of users, gauging reaction, making alterations to the technology and/or associated processes before releasing to the next tranche of users. It is usual to start the roll out with a pilot group, followed by initial groups that are well briefed in advance and are selected to provide useful feedback.

Such a launch does not create the impetus of a big bang launch, and so will generate less momentum, but for most learning technology implementations it provides the opportunity to stay close to the system users, listen to them and incorporate their feedback rapidly, making the learning technology more useful, and ideally gathering an increasing amount of support as the launch goes on. Technologically, of course, the soft launch is far safer than the big bang, where the technology must be seen to work flawlessly from the moment of launch.

The incremental launch

An incremental launch progressively increases what the learning technology offers. At Herman Miller, Jeremy Smith did a combination of a soft launch and an incremental launch. That is, he both released the EPSS to groups of users sequentially (the soft part) and progressively increased the content available after launch (the incremental part). This made the roll out fairly complex to manage, but also reduced the risk of the EPSS interrupting existing workflows – in the case of Herman Miller, that workflow was sales, the lifeblood of any enterprise. An incremental launch makes sense in instances like this, when the new system could disrupt important existing processes, also including the use of ERP, CRM and booking systems.

The 'perpetual beta'

One very successful software product – Google Mail – famously underwent a protracted beta period of five years. This softly-softly approach is the antithesis of the big bang launch. A system is put in place and trialled – usually on a voluntary basis, and usually to an invited population at first (a 'closed beta'). Then use is widened to anyone who wants to participate ('open beta'). The label 'beta' excuses almost everything while at the same time inviting the most open, useful feedback for improving the service. This and the fact that usage is optional makes it very difficult to complain about a learning technology like this. Even given the success of Google Mail, however, not every department, and not every individual, will be happy with the idea of using a product labelled as a 'beta'. Eventually, the enterprise has to be offered a final product, although with today's cloud-based software, that is a far cry from the old days of creating the 'Golden Master', the code sent to manufacturers ready for the production and shipping of disks. Today it largely means removing the word 'beta' when you are ready. (Note: this may sound similar to 'under the radar' and 'skunk works' projects. These are similar to beta products in practical terms, but very different in terms of legitimacy. We will look at them in more detail in Chapter 12.)

You may need a big bang launch with fireworks, a party, and a message from the CEO, or your 'launch' may consist only of removing the word 'beta' from a system. Whatever happens, this is just one stage in the process of implementing your learning technology. It won't stop the continued need to listen to everyone involved and to sustain your implementation.

Sustaining the implementation

The time spent initially on the Herman Miller implementation building a large, multi-disciplinary team, and the time spent subsequently in planning and gathering feedback paid off. As Jeremy puts it 'There were many minor alternations along the way but we largely stayed true to the overall course and schedule' – a retrospective view most learning technology implementers would be very happy with.

After the launch, though, the real work begins. As we saw in Chapter 7, the effort spent on maintaining a learning technology implementation should be kept to a minimum, and focused on the right sort of activities – listening to people and improving the system, rather than developing workarounds to deal with its failures. Sustaining some technologies may be a matter of general technical maintenance, but for an EPSS it is more time consuming. As Jeremy puts it: 'Sustaining the EPSS is an entirely different process and project worthy of note. An effective EPSS lives or dies by its accuracy and relevancy. To this day we are making regular updates to the tool and have an active project team, project lead, and business process to manage change.'

This is a substantial, long-term commitment of resources to the implementation. As we will see in the final part of this book, learning technologies are shifting towards closer integration with daily work, with a greater focus on immediate performance. With this change, more systems will require well-considered long-term support, bringing with it three issues, all of which have a people focus.

Resourcing

The traditional approach to internal IT projects is that they somehow are magically absorbed into daily working life post launch. Learning technologies in general are not like this, and EPSSs are certainly not like this at all, because they are in a perpetual state of change as the systems they support are updated. As these systems become increasingly cloud-based, those changes come more frequently and less predictably, because it is far easier to update software online.

Long-term maintenance of any sort needs someone's time. It is vital to make a realistic assessment of the amount of work that will be required, and to secure agreement to fund it at the start of the project. Making this assessment takes expert input from vendors, management and users. Securing the funds for maintenance needs a convincing argument as to the benefits of the approach, and a good relationship with the sponsors and stakeholders. As always, it all comes down to people and your relationship with them, and this is no trivial matter to be skimmed over in the rush to secure funding for the project as a whole. As Jeremy puts it: 'Bottom line, if you are positioning an EPSS solution, the business plan needs to include a robust sustainment strategy and long-term commitment to resources. Once you start an EPSS project, it never ends as long as the tool is in use. You never stop launching.'

That phrase is telling: 'It never ends as long as the tool is in use'. A commitment to long-term support of learning technologies is crucial. When the negotiation starts on your implementation budget, one thing should be inviolable: the resources to maintain it post-launch.

Keeping expertise engaged

Assuming that you have dealt with the first issue of resourcing, how can you ensure the maintenance is well carried out? Whether you have deployed an LMS, an EPSS or just about any other type of platform, very often the people you need to keep engaged are the Subject Matter Experts (SMEs) who helped create the initial content for that platform. The problem is that the SMEs usually see their role as part of a project that ended at launch, which is understandable, as that is how their role is normally pitched to them.

The only way to tackle this is to set out clear expectations when negotiating for SMEs' time at the start of the project. It is quite normal, for example, to request, say 10–20 hours per month of an SME's time in the run up to launch for content creation. It is far less normal to request five hours per month ongoing after launch to maintain that content, but this long-term commitment is essential. Again, this comes down to knowing your stakeholders and their drivers well, and using that information to make a persuasive case for the value of what the SMEs will be creating. The case should be there, if the project is valuable enough for the organization.

Making it happen

The final question is simple: who should be in charge of this maintenance? As learning, and learning technologies, become increasingly embedded in work, it may be that the people best suited to manage content updates are those closest to the work. This is what they did at Herman Miller where – eventually – the EPSS was maintained by a group including an internal SME, a representative of those on the CRM helpdesk, a supplier representative, and Jeremy Smith. As he puts it, maintenance 'best resides with the business unit long term rather than the learning function. We are on the team but cannot monitor the winds of change closely enough.' Up to launch and immediately after it, of course L&D must be in control, but at some point after that it makes sense to cede ongoing maintenance to those who most benefit from the technology and actually use it daily.

It might sound strange that an L&D function should effectively give up control of a major project, but ask yourself this question: where does L&D add value? The profession should be expert in enhancing performance through learning. That means ensuring the right processes and systems are in place for learning, but does not necessarily mean creating and maintaining learning content, especially if the department does not have the capacity to create enough content in a timely fashion. Sometimes the best thing L&D can do is start things running and then hand over control to the business.

A persuasive pitch

I have examined the maintenance and support of systems, because it is something too often overlooked once the technology has been launched. Now let's go right back to the beginning, to a crucial time in any implementation, requiring a very intense people focus: making the pitch to secure support for the implementations.

Obviously, those involved in successful implementations are able to pitch successfully – otherwise the project would never be approved in the first place. But a really successful pitch does far more than simply secure funding for a project, it attracts commitment and support, things that are critical during the implementation phase. Superficially designed to describe the aims of the project, great pitches also engender enthusiasm. To generate that enthusiasm, you will need to use the tools of stakeholder analysis before your pitch, so that you know what matters to each of the decision makers you face.

When Megan pitched for her LMS, she had done her homework beforehand and knew that pitching a type 2 implementation would not work. She would not get sign-off for a technology purely because it would improve the efficiency of the L&D department. Pitching it as a type 1 implementation, however, worked. Those in charge of the budget could see the benefit of risk reduction, and gave the project not only their approval, but their support.

Similarly, when Jeremy Smith made his pitch for an EPSS at Herman Miller to support the new CRM system, he was able to make the case – backed up with hard numbers – that this was the only practicable way to train people on a new system. That got the sign off. He was also able to show that this new way of learning would be less disruptive to the sales process, and so garner the active support of those signing off the project.

A successful implementation does not begin with a pitch, it begins with being able to articulate the aims of the implementation in terms that resonate with those signing it off. That in turn rests on understanding and engaging with everyone involved. This focus on understanding people feeds into another, larger attribute of successful learning technology implementations – having a wider perspective, the subject of our next chapter.

Key takeaways

1 There are at least five key groups to consider in an implementation: the L&D team, the IT department, executives and managers, partners and vendors, and those using the system.

2 To analyse your stakeholders, interview them using open questions and performance consulting techniques to establish their views of the implementation and influence on it.

3 Completing the stakeholder analysis grid as a team will help you establish where to prioritize your efforts.

4 Your communication plan can be built based on the stakeholder analysis. Be wary of 'push' messages. Effective communication relies on listening as much as telling.

5 Your pilot group should be representative of your general population. Ensure you use well-structured techniques such as Herman Miller's focus groups to gather all the feedback you can from it.

6 Your type of launch will depend on the technology you are implementing and your aims, but whatever the type, it is a key part of your communication with the organization.

7 Consider who should be responsible for sustaining the implementation post-launch. It may not be the L&D department.

8 Even in the age of the cloud, it is crucial to have good relations with the IT department. If you do not have these, begin building them immediately.

9 You will need your vendors throughout the implementation and after it. Ensure they trust you and can work with you, and with each other. If they have a 'source of reluctance' about sharing information, seek it out and address it openly.

References

Agile Alliance (2015) [accessed 12 December 2016] 12 Principles Behind the Agile Manifesto, *Agile Alliance*, 2015, [Online] https://www.agilealliance.org/agile101/12-principles-behind-the-agile-manifesto/

Applegate, L (2008) [accessed 12 December 2016] Stakeholder analysis tool, *Harvard Business Review*, Document 9-808-161, [Online] https://hbr.org/product/stakeholder-analysis-tool/808161-PDF-ENG

Bloom, N, Sadun, R and Van Reenen, J (2012) [accessed 12 December 2016] Does Management Really Work? *Harvard Business Review*, November, [Online] https://hbr.org/2012/11/does-management-really-work

LearningTechUK (2014) [accessed 8 December 2016] LSG Webinar: Using learning technologies to drive business transformation, Owen Rose, *Acteon Communications*, [Online] https://www.youtube.com/watch?v=jLoprs-UOxI

Perspective 11

The universe is wider than our views of it. HENRY DAVID THOREAU, *WALDEN*

American transcendentalist Henry Thoreau's observation, made from his cabin retreat near Concord, Massachusetts, remains as true today as when *Walden* was published in 1854. We cannot possibly understand the whole of the universe, from one viewpoint. The thought is echoed in the 1989 film *Dead Poets Society*, when teacher John Keating, played by Robin Williams, quotes Thoreau as he climbs onto the desk in front of his bemused class, adding 'I stand upon my desk to remind myself that we must constantly look at things in a different way.'

And while Thoreau was quite right about the universe, he was also right at a smaller scale. We cannot understand much at all – even our own organizations – from a single viewpoint.

The reason why this observation of Thoreau's remains relevant over a century after he made it is that we continue to ignore it. We may know it to be true in our heads, but as human beings we cannot quite believe it in our hearts. We can only ever experience the world in one way – for ourselves – and it is perfectly natural to believe that this experience represents the world in its entirety. It is natural, but fool-hardy. If we stick to this viewpoint alone, we lack the wider perspective that will increase our chances of success, a perspective we might get by standing on a desk, reflecting in a cabin in the woods or – perhaps more practically – by talking to other people and listening to their, different, viewpoint.

In Chapter 10 we explored the necessity of maintaining a strong people focus during an implementation. This idea of gaining a wider perspective on the world includes that need for people focus, but also goes beyond it. Gaining and maintaining a wide perspective is a habit that extends in time beyond a single implementation and in activity beyond soliciting opinion and feedback. It is a background activity that boosts the odds of the success of any endeavour, including implementations. On the one hand it should be a manifestation of our natural curiosity as human beings, and on the other a sensible way to avoid the pitfall of unconscious incompetence.

Unconscious incompetence – being unaware of one's own inabilities – is the enemy of any technical endeavour, including implementing a learning technology. It creates blind spots for us to blunder into, where we unexpectedly fail and are left bewildered as to why things didn't work out. Having ploughed away installing an LMS with no organizational input, the implementer wonders why usage is so poor. Having begun a programme of live online instruction, trainers wonder why people are only listening with half an ear and choosing instead to catch up on e-mail or do their expenses during class. (And, really, how boring does a class have to be if people would rather fill out their expenses while it's on?) These issues might be avoided if the implementers had started their work with a wider perspective on how and why people learned, and a real appreciation of the reality of their daily work. Having a view of the organization beyond the immediate purview of L&D does not render a practitioner immediately competent, but it does move them onto the next level – of conscious incompetence. We can never know everything we need, but if we are at least aware of where we are weak, we can call on others with greater skills and knowledge to help us.

The naivety of unconscious incompetence often correlates with inexperience, and it is notable how often successful learning technology implementations are carried out by people who have been with their organizations for a long time. Megan Garrett had been with Hershey's 16 years before her implementation, and knew enough of the complexity of her organization to gather a team around her with complementary skills and knowledge to bolster her own. Jeremy Smith started at Herman Miller in 2005 and similarly for his implementation built a wide, competent team. Experience alone, however, is not enough to give a wider perspective. Twenty years of experience is useless if it is the same year repeated 20 times. Tenure must be accompanied with a willingness to seek out new ideas, to learn new things beyond the confines of the immediate role. And when sufficiently strong, this willingness to learn trumps experience.

How willing is L&D to learn about the organization and engage with it? Some professionals are doing a great job. Unfortunately, however, there is evidence that others are far less aware of what is happening in the rest of the business.

Towards Maturity is a UK-based organization that since 2003 has been analysing how organizations move successfully towards digital learning. On the way, it has collected a considerable body of data. This has enabled Towards Maturity to show the characteristics of what it calls the 'Top Deck' of organizations, the top 10 per cent of these organizations, ranked by their level of maturity in the use of learning technology. These organizations show a consistent cluster of self-reported behaviours and characteristics.

Among the characteristics of Top Deck organizations: they are five times as likely as the bottom quartile of organizations to report a positive impact on productivity and on employee engagement. This is because they focus on outcomes rather than inputs. A traditional L&D department will measure its effectiveness by the efficiency measures of the department – in particular, by how many people have been trained over a given period. In the past this was an adequate proxy measure for success, but that is no longer the case. The L&D department in a Top Deck organization will measure its effectiveness by the extent to which it has met explicitly defined business goals.

This focus on business goals can only come from understanding what the business does, and here Top Deck organizations again outstrip the others in the survey. Before recommending a solution 92 per cent will analyse business problems (in contrast to 53 per cent of the others in the survey), 87 per cent regularly review programmes to ensure their relevance (versus 41 per cent). Most tellingly, 92 per cent say learning supports the objectives of the business. Only 62 per cent of the rest of the survey can make the same statement (Towards Maturity, 2016).

It is no coincidence that Top Deck organizations have more impact on the organization – they take the time to understand what the business goals are, and they plan to meet them. In contrast, those in the lower quartile seem to follow their own path of focusing only on what matters internally to the L&D department.

Focusing entirely on internal L&D matters is potentially fatal for a learning technologies implementation. It reduces the capacity to align activity to the business, and the willingness to seek feedback and input from others to keep that activity on track. It is not usually deliberate; only a few professionals bridle at the thought of looking outside the L&D department, but that attitude does exist. The arch proponent of the 70:20:10 model, Charles Jennings, relates the tale of the reaction of a senior L&D leader at a round table discussion with other, senior personnel from the business. As soon as the subject of business objectives was raised, she muttered 'Well that's nothing to do with me,' crossed her arms, sat back and switched off. This is an uncharacteristic reaction. Usually L&D people seek out a wider perspective, but are too time poor to maintain it.

One way of consciously striving to build and maintain a wider focus is to set in place regular routines for broadening one's perspective. Personally, I keep Friday mornings free for wider reading and aim once a month to have a face-to-face conversation with someone I would normally only encounter briefly at conferences. Others employ different strategies, but the thing is to do something, anything, to do the professional equivalent of standing on a desk and take on a different view of the world.

It is possible to consider how we see our professional environment as being defined by two dimensions – whether something is internal to the organization or beyond it, and whether something belongs within the L&D world or outside it (Figure 11.1).

This grid is a way of thinking about the subjects useful for a wide professional perspective, categorized by whether they are an issue for L&D or for the organization, and whether they are internal to the organization or external to it. The grid also shows what L&D could do in each area. It need be expert only in its own domain, but should be fully engaged with the wider professional field of L&D, connected with the rest of the business and aware of how wider trends could impact both the profession and the organization.

Keeping engaged with the wider profession is easier than ever. Social media have proved invaluable as a means of staying informed and in touch with other professionals. Other resources such as magazines, online resources, conferences and professional bodies play their part

Figure 11.1 The internal/external perspectives grid

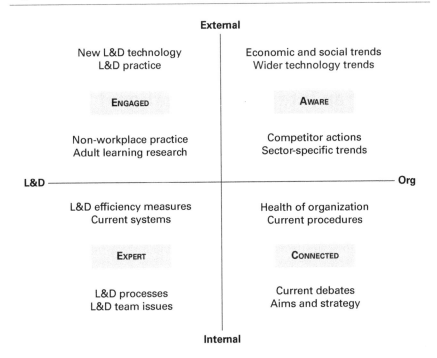

too – online and face-to-face. This wealth of material and networks mean that serious L&D professionals are always engaged, always growing their understanding of their professional field, adding to it over time, and taking it from organization to organization as their careers develop.

The same approach of reading and networking can work to stay aware of the broader social, economic and technical trends affecting L&D, as well as those bearing on employers and their particular sectors, as described in the top right quadrant.

It is quite possible, then, to keep abreast of the external matters described in the top two quadrants and serious L&D professionals are already doing this. Helpfully, staying engaged with your profession and keeping aware of developments in the wider world are both activities that can be pursued around the edges of work – whether reading in leisure hours, engaging on Twitter on the train to work or catching up with a webinar recording during a break. The tougher question lies in the bottom-right corner of the quadrant: how can

L&D professionals develop a rich understanding of their organization? This is not an activity to be followed piecemeal. It needs a well-planned approach and dedicated time.

Building an internal organizational perspective

To reiterate: gaining this rich understanding of the organization is not the same as the implementation-specific input and feedback discussed in the previous chapter, where we looked at techniques for focusing on people. It is, rather, the background knowledge that enables you to ask the right questions of those people when the project starts, the understanding that enables you to pitch the project in a way that will resonate with the business's current demands. It is the wider perspective that enables you to put the learning technology implementation into context for yourself, your department and the organization as a whole. It enables you to anticipate issues and prepare for them, rather than dealing with them as they arise.

When it comes to studying your organization, there is plenty to learn. Some of it can be done by absorbing information including company reports, earnings announcements and the marketing output of other divisions and competitors. These all provide valuable information, but part of the perspective can only be gained in one way: by getting out of the office and talking to people.

Most L&D professionals build up this understanding of how the business operates over time, by the process of their daily work bringing them into contact with a range of employees, departments and needs. But what if you do not have the luxury of time? What if you are new in the company and charged with implementing a learning technology? The answer is to accelerate the process, to use some targeted techniques to have the conversations you need.

James Tyer is a networks and community specialist who in 2015 was Global Lead of Social Collaboration for Kellogg Company. Born in England, he was based in Canada when he oversaw the implementation of a social collaboration tool across the company's 19,000 employees. With a background in L&D, James had – in previous companies – seen occasions where the training department set up an LMS and created learning content with hardly any interaction with the business, a classic case of L&D focusing entirely on its own internal affairs. When he was given the opportunity to implement Microsoft's enterprise social network Yammer across Kellogg, and a vague brief to 'make it successful', he was determined to take a very different approach, with a broader perspective.

James took the opposite approach to that taken in the hapless LMS implementation he had witnessed. New to Yammer, he started with a blank slate and began by establishing what the tool might be useful for. To do so, he took the time to interview a range of employees, establish what their work was and understand how social collaboration tools like Yammer might help them perform better. He could think of plenty of possible uses himself, from swapping client stories to sharing retail displays of Kellogg's products, but wanted to listen to what Kellogg's employees had to suggest. Over these three months, James talked to about 50 teams and departments (500–1,000 people in total) throughout the organization, at headquarters in Canada, in the UK and elsewhere. Over a conversation of 30 minutes to an hour, he discussed people's jobs with them, taking a consultative approach and spending most of his time listening to responses to the open questions he posed. In the end, he aggregated the best of the interviews and built up five or six strong cases where he thought Yammer would be a viable and useful tool.

This was no haphazard 'Build it and they will come' approach. It was a systematic approach of exploration and validation that drew heavily, says James, on the Lean Startup approach and the probe–sense–respond sequence of the Cynefin framework (Cognitive Edge, 2016).

To refine these possible use cases, he visited different departments and discussed them with groups there. Rather than begin with a talk about learning or technology, he opened with a short description of the current shift from traditional, hierarchical command and control organizations towards a looser structure (drawing in part on David Gray's *The Connected Company* and Niels Pflaeging's *Organize for Complexity*). From this starting point he would then begin a discussion around whether this view of how work was organized seemed familiar (it always did), after which he would drill down into the informal ways that people did their work. The result was almost always that participants grew excited about the possibility of having useful two-way conversations at work, the sort provided by tools like Yammer. Only then did he tie this conversation back to learning, and the idea that learning at work goes far beyond the schoolroom assumption.

As well as the general sense that communication using this tool could help individuals at their work – which he made into use cases – James also found instances where there was a specific financial advantage to using an internal mini-blogging tool. When James spoke to the VP of Marketing and Head of Marketing HR, they discussed talent development. James said that the department had spent a lot of money in previous decades on leadership development and suggested that a way of improving leadership development faster and possibly more accurately was to encourage a successful online social space where good behaviours were transparently visible and could be copied by others in the organization. The message met a positive reception.

James's odyssey of establishing how the business worked paid dividends in ways that are difficult to measure, but clearly had an impact. He established use cases for the tool, which were readily accepted as practical examples of how to use Yammer, and provided an initial user base. He also came to understand the business in a much wider sense, which helped with further promotion of the tool and indeed of learning in general. Also, his conversations acted as part of the people focus we discussed in the previous chapter. Six months into the implementation, 7,000 of the 19,000 employees were using Yammer. About half of these were directly through James's work. Directly or indirectly, the process of talking to people – and listening to them – had got people using the tool.

Someone who had been in post longer might have already had the wide understanding of the business that James acquired. But that understanding would have been developed over years. James developed his grasp of what was needed in comparatively short order, while at the same time also building up tremendous interest in the tool, a broad understanding of a complex business and an invaluable network of contacts.

There are two things to note about this experience. The first is that James was very deliberate in his process of finding out how people worked. Like an anthropologist, rather than relying on supposition, he went and talked to people about their work and observed what they actually did.

The second is that his conversations were not casual, but deliberately steered towards the topics he wanted to cover, albeit in a way that was exploratory rather than overly directive. This is no accident. There are particular techniques you can use to guide a conversation and James used them well.

Choosing to listen well

I suggested earlier in the internal/external perspectives grid (Figure 11.1) that while there is probably plenty of material to read about your organization, the best way of really understanding it is to go out and talk to people. If you invest the time to do this, it is important to use it to best effect. Like James, you have to be ready to ask the right questions and – crucially – to listen to the responses well. Asking the right initial questions is not so difficult. Most people in L&D are familiar with open questions, those that cannot be answered with a word or two. We also saw in the section on performance consulting how it is possible to be assertive and probing provided one had first established a trusting relationship.

More important than asking the right questions to start a conversation, however, is the ability to listen to what is said in reply, to listen in a way that makes the speaker feel comfortable and able to talk openly, and to provide additional short thoughts that keep the conversation going. At the end of his exploratory conversations, James Tyer reports that people often said they felt they understood their jobs better, having discussed them with him. That's the sign of a good conversation.

Leadership development consultants Jack Zenger and Joseph Folkman analysed the listening skills of nearly 3,500 managers undergoing a development programme. Looking at those judged to be great listeners by their peers, they found consistent behaviours separated them from average listeners. They grouped these behaviours into four sets:

- **Good listening means more than silence.** Of course you should give the other person your full attention and let them talk, but the best listeners do not sit silently to do this, they ask questions. These questions should not be forthright, but gently guide and probe. Good listening is more than just being receptive; it is being part of an active dialogue of joint discovery.

- **Good listening boosts the other's self-esteem.** This may have been influenced by the circumstances of the study – a leadership development programme – where managers may find themselves being stilted, critical or passive with those they are managing. Even so, as Zenger and Folkman put it, 'Good listeners made the other person feel supported and conveyed confidence in them.' You don't have to be a manager to do that, and you will engender a more open dialogue.

- **Good listening is cooperative.** In the study, poor listeners were seen as competitive, listening only for a pause in which to make their own observation, repost or criticism. Sound familiar? We do it all the time, but nobody likes being in that sort of conversation. In contrast, good listeners might challenge, probe or even disagree, but always positively, with a sense of being part of a joint enterprise.

- **Good listeners make suggestions.** This finding surprised Zenger and Folkman – after all, we know that jumping in with an unsolicited solution to a problem is never seen as helpful, what Nigel Harrison calls 'solutioneering'. They posit that perhaps it is not the act of making a suggestion itself that marks a bad listener, but the skill with which the suggestion is made (Zenger and Folkman, 2016).

As well as considering Zenger and Folkman's findings, it is always worth doing one thing frequently during your conversations: make sure you have truly understood the other person's meaning. To do this, paraphrase what they have said back to them. This prevents you walking away with a misunderstanding, or creating one during the conversation and potentially destroying the trust you have built up over the course of your dialogue. Useful ways to begin your paraphrase include:

'So, as I understand it... '

'Can I just repeat back what I think you're saying... '

'What I'm hearing you say is... '

These phrases all put the emphasis on the listener trying to get it right, rather than a phrase like 'Are you trying to say... ?' where the implication is that the correspondent has failed to express themselves adequately.

When paraphrasing, it is better not to use the exact words of your respondent. They may be invested with a particular meaning that you may miss by simply repeating them, and parroting someone's words back at them can be interpreted as being patronizing or lazy listening.

Choosing whom to talk to

Understanding your organization is partly about understanding what people do – which is what James Tyer uncovered so well during his conversations. But in any organization, performance is never just a matter of what you do, but also of whom you know. And in every organization the organization chart on the wall only tells one part of the story of where power and information can be found. Understanding the rest is a matter of uncovering the hidden power structure that lies behind the chart.

In James's research he was particularly concerned with possible uses for Yammer. As such, he was focused more on the content of conversations than anything else. If you are looking to really understand how your organization works, however, it is worth having an idea how individuals interact in an organization, and why some can be great sources of information, others may be gatekeepers enabling or blocking your progress, and still others may know exactly whom you need to contact to solve that problem of yours.

David Krackhardt is a leading researcher and thinker in the field of social networks. He is also the Professor of Organizations at the Heinz School of Public Policy and Management and the Tepper School of Business at Carnegie Mellon University. We all know that

Figure 11.2 The Krackhardt Kite Graph for a communication network

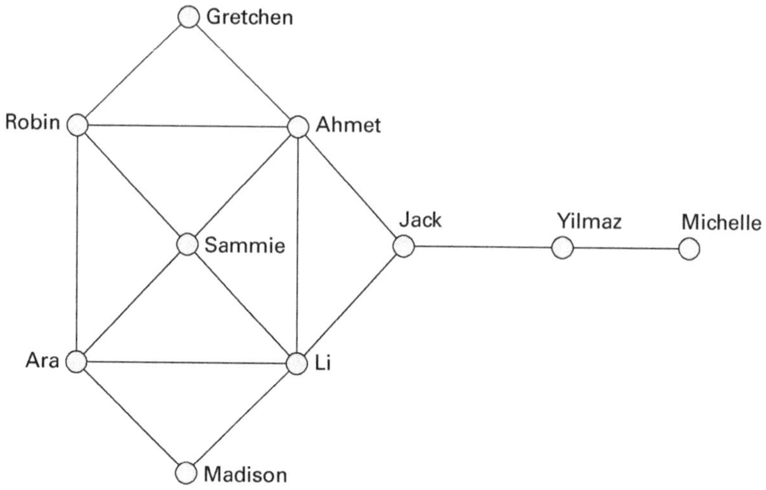

we don't work with people along the rigid lines suggested by the organizational chart. Krackhardt's great contribution has been to find a way of illustrating what actually happens between people in organizations. A simple example of this is the Krackhardt Kite Graph (Krackhardt and Hanson, 1993).

The Krackhardt Kite Graph (Figure 11.2) doesn't look much like a classic org chart, but it tells you more about what really happens in an organization, and whom you will need to deal with on different occasions.

Two nodes in the graph are connected if the people they represent communicate regularly in some way. In this graph Madison (at the bottom) communicates regularly with Li and Ara, but not with anyone else. These maps are not the product of whim, but the result of analysis of the levels of communication between people, put into numerical form and then – usually – drawn by a computer. It would not be a good use of time for anyone in L&D to map the entire social network of their organization. It is, however, well worth considering the types of people such analysis reveals.

Exploring the social networks of organizations like this has led Krackhardt and others to an idea of how people fulfil different types of role in networks. Four of the roles are:

- **Central connectors** – Sammie is highly connected, with direct links to four other people. Being a connector means she is very valuable as a source of insight into what is happening in that group. But always be aware when talking with well-connected people that even their connections have boundaries and their insights, like anyone else's, have their limits.

- **Boundary spanners** – some people may not be widely connected, but have powerful positions as the gatekeepers (or 'boundary spanners' in network terms) between groups. Here, Jack is such a powerful connector. He has only three connections, but is the guardian to Yilmaz and Michelle.

- **Information brokers** – are like boundary spanners in that they connect networks. However, unlike boundary spanners they are not always the sole connectors between networks. They do, though, always have a very wide range of indirect, or second degree, connections. Information brokers play a crucial role in effectively sharing information across social networks.

- **Peripheral specialists** – are those at the edge of a network with valuable specialist knowledge. Sometimes they are new hires trying to build connections. Sometimes they just prefer not to be overly connected. In this graph, Michelle could be a peripheral specialist (Kilduff and Krackhardt, 2008) (Cross and Prusak, 2002).

This is not an exhaustive list of the different ways in which people are connected within organizations, and it is not meant to pigeonhole employees. Nonetheless, when looking to understand how an organization works, it is worth remembering that there are such different types, and to consider the range of people you will need to talk to, as well as how to get in touch with the people you really need.

Suppose that Michelle is indeed a peripheral specialist. She may have valuable insight into a technical matter of potential use in a future learning technology implementation. What is the best way to reach her? You could pick up the phone or send an e-mail, but it is usually better to approach people via a trusted intermediary. In this case Yilmaz (or Jack) would be a good first step.

And when you talk to Michelle, you won't be talking to her just once. You will be forging a relationship with her that you can call on again in the future, if needs be. Someone in the modern L&D department must play the role of trusted information broker, well connected via second-degree connections across the network. Remember how Jeremy Smith stayed in contact with his internal IT department and external vendors so that he was able to solve technical issues when they cropped up a long time after launch? It is likely that your learning technology implementation will rely on that wide, loose network of allies, so start building it today.

When building a wide network of allies, do so in a spirit of useful contribution. Fortunately in L&D we should always have something helpful to offer, particularly around information and tips on improving productivity or just interesting stuff to read. The point is, as always, that starting a conversation focused on one's own needs ('I'd like to hear about your work') is seldom as exciting a conversation as one which is collaborative and mutually beneficial ('Let's talk about your work and how I may be able to help you').

Perspective via experience

One way of gaining a wider perspective is to see the business through the eyes of others, which is the approach James Tyer took. An alternative is to gain an understanding of the business directly through experience. And the best type of experience for this is often when things do not go to plan.

One person who learned a lot from experience about implementing learning technology was someone we will call Jim Jones, an eLearning Manager in Flight Operations for a large airline that will remain nameless. When Jim joined the airline in 2010 he brought with him a wealth of experience in design, technology and learning to an organization that was already using technology in learning. Airlines were early adopters of Computer Based Training (CBT) in the 1990s, but as e-learning became established at the turn of the millennium, many decided that it was time to move to an LMS. The move made sense from the point of functionality and cost effectiveness, but like any technology change, it had to be planned, managed and executed well.

It was the first true LMS that this airline had chosen, and it went through a six-month implementation process, transferring over personnel data and courses from the old CBT system. In June 2012 the system went live. Not long after that, the issues started.

Airlines split their businesses into branches, such as Flight Operations, which deals with the crew flying the planes, and Customer Service Operations, which includes everything to do with passengers, from in-flight crew, gate agents to baggage handlers to customer service personnel. It became clear very quickly that the LMS selected, while fine for Customer Service Operations, was not suitable for staff in Flight Operations.

Employees in Customer Service Operations were able to use the LMS as it was designed to be used – at a desk, on a workstation, often in a classroom set aside for the purpose in the airline's offices. Here the IT team would be able to set up the PC according to the LMS requirements. In contrast, almost all flight operations personnel – pilots, flight crew – are perpetually on the move, and they wanted to use a range of machines and mobile devices to learn from, whether in the office, at home or in a hotel. This was no trivial inconvenience. Jim estimated that before the launch about 5 per cent of the team's time was spent on IT user support. After launch that jumped to 75 per cent.

The root cause of these issues was straightforward. Although Flight Operations backed the tendering process, and believed that the LMS purchased was a good one, the whole process was driven by the Customer Service Operations and neither of the two branches had been involved previously in either tendering for an LMS, or implementing one. The result was that the purchasing team did not have the wide perspective needed on how all employees worked. They had not considered how very different the learning environment would be for Flight Operations staff and – crucially – they had not thought to find out. It was a classic case of not knowing what you don't know.

The difficulties that the LMS created, however, catalysed both L&D teams. Within six months they had reassessed their needs and produced a Request for Proposals (RFP) checklist for a new system with over a hundred items on it. Here's how Jim described this when we spoke:

... once we were ready to start going to RFP it really came down to that major point... you have to know your business. You have to have a deep understanding of your training culture. At this point we were really able to grasp what worked in the past, what failed in the past and why did it fail. We had to really know our own strengths, our own weaknesses.

It would be hard to find a more graphic description of the need for perspective than this. As Jim puts it: 'You have to know your business.' From that understanding, they were able to draw up this extensive RFP checklist, which included legal requirements as well as functional. For example, the new LMS would have to have its data centre located in the same country as the airline, for regulatory reasons (the previous one had not). It had to be cloud-based; anything else would be impractical for an airline with staff potentially spread over several countries. Functionally, the LMS had to enable a member of the flight crew to take a course on any device – including any mobile device – then pick up the course later, on a different device, and start at the same place.

The process of building out the RFP checklist enabled them to be proactive with their potential suppliers. For example, although one supplier seemed to offer a good solution, there was a potential problem with its use of pop-up windows. Because the tendering team knew the issues involved in some detail they were able to brief the supplier, which set about rewriting some fundamental parts of their code base and were able to return in two months with a solution. They won the contract.

The experience not only shaped how the airline chose an LMS for current needs, it also made the tendering team acutely aware that any system would have to be able to adapt in the foreseeable future – from one to five years ahead. They were realistic enough to know that no system could offer what had yet to be invented, but they wanted to know that the company had the foresight to be planning for new developments, and that the software could – where possible – connect into other systems that might offer, in particular, Virtual Reality and Augmented Reality (AR) content. This focus on new technology was not fanciful; it was based on the airline industry's history as an early adopter of tools that enable more productive working. Boeing announced it was working on specialist AR kit as far back as 2006 (Boeing, 2006).

Did the wider perspective pay off? Absolutely. The second implementation was completed in 40 days rather than 6 months, and while there was a minor uptick in helpdesk calls after launch, it was nothing near the leap experienced with the previous implementation. Jim puts this success down to a combination of setting the right RFP upfront, relentless, brutal testing prior to launch, and having the right team on board, lined up, fully briefed and ready to work on the implementation in a way that was completely absent in the first implementation.

Ultimately, Jim was very clear: it all comes down to knowing the business and extending your perspective beyond your own. As he put it: 'If you don't understand or know your business then you're not going to get very far. You'll have to bring in those resources or those people that know that bit.'

Everyone has setbacks, but not everyone learns from them. Clearly Jim Jones and the airline learned from their initial LMS implementation in two ways. The first lesson was a very practical one and produced the RFP checklist. This not only made selecting the second LMS easier, the process of producing the checklist helped them focus on and truly understand the learning needs of the entire organization. That in turn helped them create and execute their very successful project plan – a 40-day roll out is impressively tight for a large, widely dispersed enterprise like an airline. In producing the checklist, they were helped by the airline industry's long tradition of successfully using checklists, noted by Atul Gawande in *The Checklist Manifesto* (Gawande, 2011). Not all enterprise cultures are as successful at developing and using checklists – including Gawande's own field of medicine.

In most implementations, this extensive RFP checklist would have been developed during an initial phase – what I have called the 'Understanding' step in Chapter 7, and what many implementers call the 'Discovery' phase. It was not, however, produced for their first LMS. The decision to create it afterwards was a result of the second, more profound, lesson: that a wide perspective is crucial for a successful implementation. When Jim Jones said 'You'll have to bring in… those people that know' and Henry David Thoreau said 'The universe is wider than our views of it', they were saying the same thing.

Learning from one's own experience is effective, but the lessons can be hard won. Learning from others' experience is not as vivid but it is faster and less painful. Thanks to social media and the web connecting us to people and information, it is easier than ever today to learn from others. That is both a blessing and a curse. It should enable us to consider things we might have otherwise overlooked. But this superabundance of information must also carry a note of caution. It provides an excellent opportunity for a discovery phase that never ends, for 'paralysis by analysis', in H Igor Ansoff's memorable phrase.

Jim Jones' airline saw its Understanding phase as the means to an end – getting an LMS bought, configured and deployed. The work the airline did enabled them to gain the perspective they needed, and there was something else about it that matters for this book. The L&D team's emphasis on focused action is the very opposite of paralysis by analysis, and is one of the defining characteristics of the last of our four characteristics of success. That characteristic is the one that gets the job done on time and to budget. It is the team's Attitude.

Key takeaways

1 Unconscious incompetence – not knowing what you don't know – is one of the great traps for a technology implementation. To avoid it, consciously develop the wider perspective of your team.

2 The internal/external perspectives grid gives prompts of some topics to consider in gaining that wider perspective on both L&D and the business.

3 If you are new to an organization, consider the interview approach taken by James Tyer in building use cases for a learning technology.

4 Listening effectively is essential when conversing with the business. The research of Zenger and Folkman and others gives useful hints on developing this powerful skill.

5 You don't have to produce an organizational network map for your employer, but must consider a wide range of people to build bonds with, and how to reach them.

6 Building an internal perspective of your organization should be a long-term project. Spread the responsibility across your team and have regular meetings to discuss what each member has learned from the people they have spoken to.

7 Learning from experience is essential, and is most effective when that learning is consciously pursued and the learning well-articulated, as with Jim Jones' airline implementation.

References

Boeing (2006) [accessed 14 December 2016] Now See This, *Boeing Frontiers*, October, [Online] http://www.boeing.com/news/frontiers/archive/2006/october/i_ids03.pdf

Cognitive Edge (2016) [accessed 14 December 2016] Making sense of complexity in order to act, *Cognitive Edge*, [Online] http://cognitive-edge.com/

Cross, R and Prusak, L (2002) [accessed 14 December 2016] The People Who Make Organizations Go—or Stop, *Harvard Business Review*, June, [Online] https://hbr.org/2002/06/the-people-who-make-organizations-go-or-stop

Gawande, A (2011) *The Checklist Manifesto: How to get things right*, Profile Books, London

Kilduff, M and Krackhardt, D (2008) *Interpersonal Networks in Organizations: Cognition, personality, dynamics, and culture*, Cambridge University Press, Cambridge

Krackhardt, D and Hanson, J (1993) [accessed 14 December 2016] Informal Networks: The company behind the chart, *Harvard Business Review*, July–August, [Online] https://hbr.org/1993/07/informal-networks-the-company-behind-the-chart

Towards Maturity (2016) *Unlocking Potential: Releasing the potential of the business and its people through learning, 2016–17 Learning Benchmarking Report*, Towards Maturity, p 74

Zenger, J and Folkman, J (2016) [accessed 14 December 2016] What Great Listeners Actually Do, *Harvard Business Review*, July, [Online] https://hbr.org/2016/07/what-great-listeners-actually-do

Attitude 12

When Kelly rolled up his sleeves, he became unstoppable... He declared his intention, then pushed through. BEN R RICH, SKUNK WORKS

Le mieux est l'ennemi du bien.
(The best is the enemy of the good.) VOLTAIRE, LA BÉGUEULE

Time and again in successful implementations I have seen a particular attitude exhibited by a team that refused to let anything stand in the way of a good deployment. I would include in that Jim Jones's airline, which rapidly responded to its poor initial implementation with an excellent second one. Of course, the word 'attitude' has many meanings. I don't mean a sassy or negative attitude. Neither do I mean a conveniently vague collection of psychological traits. I mean a particular approach to work that encompasses the following:

- a laser-like focus on the aims of the project;
- a predisposition towards taking action;
- a willingness to listen and to be challenged;
- pragmatism and the ability to compromise;
- an openness to risk.

Looking at the first of these, we have seen in previous chapters some of the various techniques that can be used to clarify the aims of an implementation. In successful projects, this is naturally coupled with the second point: a predisposition to action. Similarly, while we explored the methods for engaging with people in the chapters on People and Perspective, there is no point doing that if the team will not listen to what is said, especially if it is challenging, the third point.

The last two points on the list above – pragmatism and openness to risk – have not been dealt with previously, however, yet these are the essential parts of the right attitude. They make everything else possible.

The art of pragmatic compromise

Teams running successful implementations are, above all, pragmatic. The team is focused on reaching its goal, true, but knows that most of the time this can only be attained by compromise along the way. Voltaire's epithet at the beginning of this chapter captures that thought neatly. Usually translated as 'the perfect is the enemy of the good', it is a reminder that if you wait for perfection in anything – content design, stakeholder analysis, deployment planning – you will never roll out anything. The trick is to strike the right balance. Plan for everything and you will never start. Start without a plan and you will fail. Think of the LMS implementations of Megan Garrett and Jim Jones (the second, successful implementation!) and of Jeremy Smith's EPSS deployment. These were the result of well-structured planning that did not wait for all the answers before starting.

Of course, great implementers know you cannot compromise on everything. Jeremy Smith compromised on a number of things when implementing the EPSS at Herman Miller, including rewriting his team's communications agreement during the implementation. One area he would not have compromised on, however, was the need for dedicated support post-launch, something he saw as essential to the long-term success of the project. Similarly, Jim Jones would not have compromised on equal access to the LMS for all staff in his airline.

What is the source of this ability to both focus on the end goal and strike the right compromises along the way to it? It seems to be a matter of experience, experience that can be shared across team members or largely accumulated in the hands of the team leader. Combine that experience with an acceptance of a certain level of risk and a propensity to take action and you have the basis for the right attitude.

Risk, decisions and judgement

Risk-aversion will hinder any significant implementation. It hampers compromise, because the risk-averse see compromise as introducing uncertainty (rather than what it usually is: the only way to make progress). It hampers decision-making, because any decision carries the risk of being wrong. Furthermore, and even worse for the risk-averse, most decisions in an implementation must be made with incomplete information. Faced with this, the typical risk-averse reaction is to clarify the decision-making process by seeking out more information. This is seldom effective. In contrast, successful teams rely on their judgement to make the best calls they can with the information they have at the time.

While any learning technology implementation involves a series of tactical decisions like this, they all ask four, high-level questions. These can be framed in terms of the four APPA characteristics (Figure 12.1).

Of these four, we have seen how to clarify the aim of the project ('Why?'), the people involved ('Who?') and the perceived context ('What?'). In these areas, tools like performance consulting, stakeholder analysis and building personal networks reduce risk. It is the attitude towards the implementation ('How?') that carries the most uncertainty. Here, there are innumerable tough decisions to be made, with incomplete information and sometimes no good answer, only a less bad one. In the detail of implementation, most decisions will be made by the team, but the toughest calls are where the team leadership proves itself.

Figure 12.1 APPA: four characteristics and questions

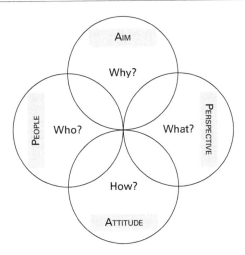

The role of leadership

On a large implementation, it is rare to find one person capable of covering all this alone, hence my emphasis on the team throughout this book. Smart leaders, of course, ensure their teams cover each piece of APPA. When Megan was running the LMS implementation for Hershey's, she found her project manager invaluable for keeping the implementation focused on hitting project milestones. Jeremy Smith's implementation at Herman Miller featured a team of 22 to make sure every aspect of the implementation was covered.

But while it is possible to distribute tasks across a team, a great deal of research has gone into what makes up successful project management and delivery, and much of this research supports the role of the team leader in critical in delivering project success. For example:

> All the evidence of recent research supports the idea that successful projects are led by individuals who possess not only a blend of technical and management knowledge, but also leadership skills that are internally compatible with the motivation of the project team and externally compatible with client focus strategies. (Hyväri, 2006)

Leadership of the team, then, is crucial to success and probably at least as important as the management of the project itself.

Where does the ability to run a project well come from? A considerable amount of it probably comes from experience. Hyväri (2006) notes that in successful projects there is a strong correlation between a project manager's total work experience and the commitment of end users to the project. Many of the judgement calls, the compromises, which have to be made along the course of an implementation are best made against the backdrop of previous experience.

And if the leader of the team does not have the right experience at any point, then he or she must show the right leadership by allowing space for members of the team to contribute their experience before deciding when to move on.

One of the areas in which the leader has to show the ability to compromise well is in balancing the conflicting demands of the four different characteristics of a successful implementation (Figure 12.2).

Figure 12.2   APPA: tensions between the characteristics

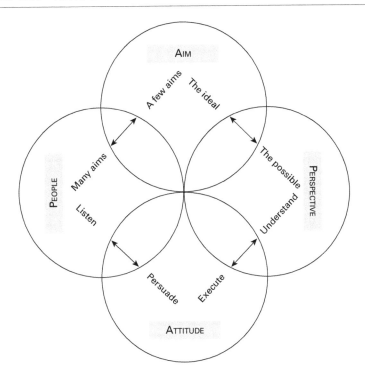

If the team has the right attitude, it will be focused on execution. While this supports the four APPA characteristics, it is also one source of tension between them. As we noted at the end of the previous chapter, one's perspective is always under development. This will always be in conflict with the drive to finish the job on time. Similarly, the focus on completion will lead team members to want to persuade people to adopt a project. The people-focused approach, however, will typically want to listen to people to understand their take on the technology.

There are other tensions, too. People within an organization will always have their own, individual aims that they want to achieve, while the project can only succeed if it has one or two clear aims. And while there may be an ideal aim for the use of a learning technology, this always has to be tempered by the context of the organization into what is actually possible to achieve.

These tensions are natural in any project. It is the job of the team leader to draw on his or her own experience and that of the team to balance them and make the best call for the project.

Kelly Johnson and the Skunk Works

One person who epitomizes both great leadership and a goal-focused attitude was the aeronautical engineer Clarence 'Kelly' Johnson, an aircraft designer for Lockheed, although to call him just an aircraft designer is to understate the achievement of a man responsible for the Lockheed U-2 spy plane and the SR-71 Blackbird, a plane so advanced that it has held the record for the fastest air-breathing manned aircraft in the 40 years since 1976 (Wikipedia, 2016). (To put that in perspective, the previous three aircraft held the record for 14 years between them.)

As Ben R Rich noted in the quote used at the beginning of this chapter, Kelly was notable for his single-minded drive towards accomplishing his goal, but on the way he didn't mind being proved wrong, as he was occasionally, if it helped push the project along. He lost a bet to Rich on the benefits of using a particular paint for the SR-71. Having thought about the matter overnight he returned to the office the next day, and told Rich, simply: 'On the black paint, you were right about the advantages and I was wrong' and he handed him the amount of their wager: a quarter. The result was the characteristic colour for the plane, a reduced radar profile and its nickname, the Blackbird. More importantly, from our point of view, was the way Johnson dealt with this issue. Although he had been opposed to using this particular paint, he was convinced by the facts presented to him, prepared to concede and to move on with the project. It was entirely in keeping with his direct approach to project management. Kelly was one of the first, if not the first, to use the maxim KISS – Keep It Simple, Stupid (Rich and Janos, 1995).

We tend to glorify individuals – and Kelly Johnson rightly collected a massive slew of awards during his lifetime – but Kelly and others would agree that their achievements could only ever have been achieved through a team. He thought a lot about the process of engineering and running his team, and boiled his thinking down to Kelly's 14 Rules and Practices. These rules emphasize much of what we have discussed, including trust, timeliness, authority to act and quality of team members. From rule 5, it seems that Kelly managed the combined balancing act for discipline and speed that we would today consider part of an Agile approach. The rule is also an exemplary piece of pragmatic compromise in itself:

> There must be a minimum number of reports required, but important work must be recorded thoroughly. (Lockheed, 2016a)

Kelly was celebrated, though, not just for his achievements and his approach, but for running a department that has given its name to similar groups elsewhere: the Skunk Works. (The Lockheed Martin website tells the fascinating tale of the 1943 origins of the term skunk works, based on a deadline, a circus tent and a newspaper cartoon.) (Lockheed, 2016b)

A skunk works is a place in the organization where things happen in a sort of grey area of official sanction. Management turns a blind eye to what is going on based on its trust of the skunk works leadership. While large projects such as LMS or EPSS implementations typically do not start in a skunk works, smaller projects frequently do, and when talking to people with the right attitude, the phrases 'skunk works', 'guerrilla project' and 'under the radar' occur surprisingly regularly. Other commonly used phrases include 'seeking forgiveness rather than permission' and 'going rogue'.

Going 'semi-rogue'

When I Skyped Geoff Stead for our interview he was sitting on a deck, overlooking the Pacific Ocean, on a beautiful Californian morning. Although he has since relocated back to England, at the time Geoff lived close to his then employers, Qualcomm, the manufacturers of the key components for most modern smartphones, with a global workforce of over 30,000 people.

Geoff reported directly to the chief learning officer (CLO) and ran a team inside the HR function, supporting, but not reporting to, the corporate learning team. His team of 15 covered a mixture of design, e-learning and mobile technical development.

Recruited specifically to innovate internally and support effective working with mobile devices, Geoff and his team were responsible for developing and commissioning many enterprise learning and performance support apps. This in itself was challenging given the lack of existing mobile learning apps designed for enterprises, but even more challenging was the complexity of distributing apps in a safe, secure manner to a very global, very diverse workforce that used a wide range of devices. There was no official way to do this.

In an ideal world, application distribution would be managed by IT, but unfortunately Qualcomm's mobile learning ambitions were several years ahead of the market, meaning there was a mismatch between what IT could support on their mobile roadmap (which had a focus on enterprise services), and those aspired to by the CLO (who wanted a self-service app store of enterprise apps, available to all employees). IT were sympathetic to the idea, but were several years away from being able to implement or support one. This looked like a major impasse between the aims of the two departments.

With characteristic British understatement, Geoff described this as 'a slightly awkward position', given that he had been recruited specifically to embed mobile into the workplace. Together with the CLO he decided that the business benefits of mobile couldn't wait, so worked with his team to build their own internal app store for employees – a self-service site where people could find tools for performance support, learning and anything else they needed for their jobs.

HR and L&D do not typically lead on technology developments, so to succeed required reaching out to other innovators across the business to deal with issues beyond their control such as security clearance and server access. Geoff's team had solid technical credentials, so were able to build strong links to teams within the IT department charged with evaluating future technologies. This worked well, as both teams were able to test out ideas on each other. It also meant that when the IT department was ready to transition these ideas into business as usual, the L&D platform was aligned with their plans. This turned out to be a pragmatic, supportive and transparent working relationship. With the help of this particular part of the IT department, Geoff's team got on with developing and deploying the app store, within the CLO's timescale.

When I put it to Geoff that this was a great example of going rogue, because his team was effectively working outside the official IT roadmap, he demurred. It was, he pointed out, aligned with what the CLO wanted and with what the research teams within IT wanted. The implementation was just a little ahead of its time. Furthermore, it was totally aligned with the enterprise goals. It was, Geoff said, 'more semi-rogue'. My take is that for many L&D professionals, working on a technology project without the prior approval of the head of IT would have seemed 100 per cent rogue; two reasons make it seem only 'semi-rogue' to Geoff. The first is the company culture. Like many engineering-based firms, there was a strong tradition in Qualcomm of trying things out, of having a go. Ultimately, this supportive culture created a climate that made producing the app store possible. But the second reason is that this is Geoff's own attitude, and that of his team. They believed it was the right thing to do for the business, and had full support of the CLO. Having been charged with making it happen, like Kelly Johnson, he did.

The app store went on to be hugely successful as the core channel to useful mobile information. Initially it was seen as an L&D platform, but quickly expanded to be the central place for all things mobile, which raised and positively altered the profile of the L&D department.

Perhaps inevitably, the store enabled further instances of going 'semi-rogue'. One group of interns were so frustrated with getting lost on the company's many campuses that they set up a mapping app allowing employees to navigate the offices, call shuttles and locate different buildings. That app has gone on to become one of the store's most popular.

What made it possible to rapidly develop and deploy this platform for internal knowledge sharing despite the seemingly impossible odds? The answer:

- **Trust and respect:** Based on existing shared skills and ethos, Geoff's team were able to work openly with the IT team without having to forge any mutual understanding.

- **Skilled personnel**: Geoff's team had the skills to complete most of the job themselves. When necessary they could call on advice from the IT team and other experts.

- **A clear task, with perspective:** Geoff had a close partnership with the CLO, who had been in the business for many years, and was able to see the bigger picture, and overarching business priorities. Combining that with strong technology skills kept the right balance between vision and practical solution.

- **Data-driven execution**: An app store would not build its own traffic. Once it was built, the team populated it with a good many apps, and relentlessly examined usage data, modifying the store, adding apps and running promotional campaigns to ensure constant, ongoing improvements. With more than 24,000 users accessing it, the only meaningful way to get feedback was via analytics.

- **Business alignment:** The apps with most usage were not classic learning apps, but were apps designed around clear business challenges. Sometimes workflow improvement, sometimes reference guides, sometimes simple aggregators of internal systems notifications. This clear alignment with current business plan points helped the L&D team transition into a role of deeper business support.

Context, perspective and attitude

When Geoff Stead and his team were given a tough task by his CLO, they solved the issue by going semi-rogue, and working with colleagues internally to develop and deliver a complex technical answer to it. It was a unique problem, and they had to find their own unique solution to it.

While Geoff's case may seem unusual, every learning technology implementation is unique. It is just unusual for this to be as starkly clear as it was with Geoff's team. Every implementation has its own particular context and this is why trying to complete a learning technologies implementation by rote, by going through a series of stages rigidly, is never enough. This is not to say that process and planning are not important. A process such as the six stages outlined in Chapter 7 is essential, but not sufficient. The process has to be adapted to the unique circumstances of a particular implementation. Making that adaptation takes the right pragmatic attitude.

Back in Chapter 8 we looked at a detailed case study of a successful LMS implementation at Hershey's that exemplified each of the four characteristics in APPA. We will close this part of the book with an examination of a learning technology programme that again shows APPA in use, and which exemplifies the value of the right attitude in getting the job done.

Going your own way

When Nick Shackleton-Jones joined energy company BP in December 2010 as Head of Online and Informal Learning, he had come from a similar role at the BBC, and he brought with him clear ideas of what was effective in learning. It was different from what he found in his new workplace.

At the time, BP had about 80,000 full-time and 80,000 contractor staff, spread over 80 countries, and 6,000 new joiners a year. These new hires went through a blended induction programme that included eight hours of e-learning modules, but the training was not an attractive proposition, with only a few hundred new hires making use of it annually. The problem, as described by Nick, was two-fold. The first was logistics. Given the size of the company, many people received no induction until weeks or months after joining, when it was far less useful. The second was the quality of the material, which Nick calls 'a dire experience'. It focused on business content, not what employees might actually need on a new job and it was pushed out in a dry, e-learning format (Bersin, 2015).

Nick saw an opportunity to change things. The pitch for his project was a combination of type 2 and type 3 proposals. Yes, the new approach would work better – a fully online solution would be far more cost- and time-efficient than a blended one, especially for such a dispersed organization (type 2). But, in addition, it would shift the focus to effective performance support, enabling people to get up to speed in their new roles faster (type 3). To create buy-in for this approach, Nick produced a 'destination postcard', a mock-up of what the new programme would look like. The new approach would be an engaging introduction to BP that would confirm new recruits' decision to join the company and let them be useful sooner. Senior management bought into the vision of something exciting and different and gave the project their support.

What was in this new programme? Rather than a course pushing out a collection of dry facts about the business, Nick and his team wanted a set of resources that people could pull down to tackle the challenges and contexts that new joiners typically faced in an easily accessible, and well produced mix of formats. The site should resemble the kinds of tools new joiners were already using in their personal lives, rather than conventional corporate education. The first step in the project was to understand what new hires actually wanted and needed to know. Like Herman Miller's Jeremy Smith in Chapter 10, Nick brought people together in groups and listened to them.

For what Nick and his team called audience analysis, they conducted 12 focus groups of up to 15 new starters about three months into their jobs, meeting face-to-face to describe 'the emotional curve' of their time immediately after joining. This created a graph of highs and lows over time. This approach 'showed where people were excited and engaged, where they were down and feeling stupid or even considering quitting. The discussion told us why they felt that way'. New joiners typically felt that they were being asked both to absorb a lot of new information, and to adapt to a new culture at the same time. In addition, the team asked new joiners to list the top 10 tasks and concerns that they confronted during onboarding, providing a statistical basis for the subsequent design. Many said that what they needed to know was either absent entirely (such as 'common mistakes') or embedded in other systems, rather than being accessible at their point of need (Bersin, 2015). It was, in short, produced at the convenience of the course producer rather than to meet the needs of the employee.

These focus groups enabled Nick and his team to see how learning could improve time to autonomy, the crucial metric for onboarding. Dumping content on people is not an effective way of doing this. Rather, the new onboarding approach sought to answer the questions people have when they join any organization: 'They want to fit in, like on their first day at school. They want to know where to go and what to do, and they don't want to make silly mistakes.'

The focus groups uncovered a spectrum of needs from new hires' emotional concerns to their practical needs. Once these are uncovered, it is possible to match content to each need. As Nick describes it: 'The emotional concerns are often best dealt with using video. For concerns like "How do I show up, what do I wear" we just had people record honest, unscripted videos of "What it's like in my part of BP". They were immensely popular, and reassuring. The practical stuff is very often best dealt with using straightforward tools like checklists which spell out what you need to do over the course of your first week.'

Dealing with the practical side helped people do their jobs better. Addressing the emotional side also helped by building confidence and enabling them to learn more, and do more, faster.

To keep stakeholders on board, the team held a limited number of review meetings (about 24 over eight months), giving them a chance to see and comment on a prototype. Those invited included: HR business partners, training colleagues, brand managers, the legal department and others. Nick describes this as 'a wide and challenging group of stakeholders' – and this is a classic case of good stakeholder management, seeking out the difficult conversations rather than staying in the comfort zone of only conversing with people already committed to the project. Using the input from the target audience and feedback from stakeholders, they had a content portal in place within eight months, called *Discover BP*.

The content on the portal was clear and context-sensitive, making it possible for new employees to find what they needed at their moment of need. (We find ourselves returning again to this phrase of Mosher and Gottfredson.) To make the content as useful as possible, there was a very strong focus on the quality of design and the user experience – content was not dry 'click-next' e-learning, but accessible videos, animations, infographics, checklists and other resources that people could put to use immediately. Production values were as high as possible for each piece, and the content was designed typically to be short enough to be completed in its entirety at the point of need. This was the epitome of something that Nick Shackleton-Jones has long espoused: a move from courses to resources, and very far from the frustrations of Sally in Starbucks, whom we met at the beginning of Chapter 1.

This could have been the moment for a glitzy launch, but Nick was quite clear about something. In a company the size of BP 'it is never possible to get all the stakeholders involved'. To deal with this, the team soft-launched *Discover BP* as a beta product. 'If you keep the product in perpetual beta, people can't be outraged that they haven't been consulted. They still have the chance to contribute.'

It turned out that there were snags to be fixed, and ongoing ways in which the product could be extended and enhanced, very much along the iterative approach of the Shewhart/Deming PDCA cycle that we met in Chapter 7. In doing so, as always, it was the people who were paramount: 'These are all important issues, but are all technical issues. In principle these issues are always solvable. In practice, they are intractable without the relationships.'

After the soft launch, the L&D team ran a six-month multichannel campaign to generate awareness, including webinars, videos, regular mentions on the BP intranet, posters and – of course – e-mail.

The usefulness of the resources, combined with the awareness campaign, meant that *Discover BP* became the most heavily used area on the company's intranet, with a million page impressions in the first three and a half years of use – vastly more than can be accounted for by new joiners alone. Over that period, more than 200,000 learning sessions have been run, and by Nick's calculation, over half the people in BP have used it.

This level of usage is something most people in learning technology can only dream of. One of the perennial topics at the Learning Technologies Conference in London – and, indeed, at most conferences concerned with learning technology – is how to improve adoption rates of systems and content. For Nick, that is putting the question the wrong way around. 'If you have to ask "How do I get people to use my e-learning?" then you're asking the wrong question', he says. 'If it's useful, and the communications strategy is right, then people will use it. By building content for people starting at BP we have solved problems for everyone working at BP, which is why it continues to be used.'

We explored in Chapter 9 a range of ways of measuring the value or impact of a learning intervention. For an onboarding package like this, the classic approach would be to understand how quickly new recruits had reached competence, and to compare this with the pre-intervention baseline. In this instance such an approach was impractical. BP was hiring into a vast range of roles, each affected by unique local conditions. More importantly, such an approach to value was simply not necessary. The key measure of value for any implementation is whether it meets its business goals. *Discover BP* did – hitting both the efficiency goal of delivering content better to an international audience, and on anecdotal and usage evidence, clearly meeting the effectiveness goal of enthusing new joiners and reducing their time to autonomy.

L&D often believes, erroneously, that a hard ROI measure is the only way to be taken seriously in the business. The *Discover BP* programme gives the lie to that. Success comes from being clear about goals and being seen to meet them, as Nick explains. 'Once we'd built Discover BP, everything changed. From being recruited to more or less sit in the corner and mind the LMS, I had people coming up to me and asking "How can we do that?" For the first time, senior executives were interested in, and excited by, e-learning. They truly believed we were at the forefront of driving innovation and change in the learning space in BP.'

Rebels with a cause

In the 1953 movie when asked, 'Hey, Johnny, what you rebelling against?' Johnny Strabler, played by Marlon Brando, answers 'Whaddaya got?' For many people, this is 'attitude' – a vague, directionless rebellion. When I use the word 'attitude', it is to describe something far more focused. The attitude that Nick Shackleton-Jones and his team showed at BP, like Geoff Stead at Qualcomm, was the same shown by all the successful implementations in this book. They use their cumulative experience to judge when they have enough information to move forwards – balancing project deadlines against potential risk at each stage, and accepting that risk can never be reduced to nothing. This is how they pragmatically reconcile the clear purpose of the project with the necessity of change as the implementation progresses.

Unlike Brando's Johnny Strabler, smart learning technology implementers are not really rebels, or if they are, they are rebels with a cause – the cause of getting L&D right, despite the schoolroom assumption that learning is only about putting information in front of people.

Throughout Part Two of this book we have explored the idea that a good learning technologies implementation has four characteristics – a clear Aim, a People focus, a broad Perspective and the right Attitude. In the last chapter of the book, where we examine the future roles of L&D, we will explore the future of the profession in the light of these four characteristics. First, though, there is an essential question to be answered: Will tomorrow's workplace learning technologies be a continuation of today's, or can we expect something new, and if so, what will it be?

The attitude underpinning successful learning technology implementations is defined by focus, a bias towards action, an openness to being challenged, a willingness to compromise pragmatically and an openness to risk.

Key takeaways

1 'Risk' is not the same as the randomness of 'chance'. Accepting risk means accepting that no implementation can be free of the danger of failure, and being willing to act with imperfect information, a necessity in any technical implementation.

2 Taking action despite incomplete information requires a willingness to compromise. Research suggests that the best way of learning how to compromise and make other tough decisions is through experience.

3 The four APPA characteristics effectively ask four questions of the implementation: Why are we doing this? Who is involved? What is the context? And how will we make it happen?

4 Conflict between these four questions is inevitable, and can only be resolved by drawing on the experience of the implementation team and its leader. The ultimate criterion in making these decisions is whether it advances the project at an acceptable level of risk.

5 Our two case studies in this chapter explored implementations which could have been seen as risky from the outside, but which both team leaders saw as in the best interests of the organization as a whole.

References

Bersin (2015) Point-of-need, Continuous, New-hire Learning: How BP redesigned the onboarding experience to engage employees and enable continuous learning, *Dani Johnson*, June, Bersin by Deloitte

Hyväri, I (2006) [accessed 12 December 2016] Success of Projects in Different Organizational Conditions, *Project Management Journal*, September, [Online] http://csbweb01.uncw.edu/people/rosenl/classes/OPS100/Success%20of%20Projects%20in%20Different%20Organizational%20conditions.pdf

Lockheed (2016a) [accessed 12 December 2016] Kelly's 14 Rules & Practices, [Online] http://www.lockheedmartin.com/us/aeronautics/skunkworks/14rules.html

Lockheed (2016b) [accessed 12 December 2016] Skunk Works® Origin Story, [Online] http://www.lockheedmartin.com/us/aeronautics/skunkworks/origin.html

Rich, B R and Janos, L (1995) *Skunk Works: A personal memoir of my years at Lockheed*, Time Warner Paperback, London

Wikipedia (2016) [accessed 12 December 2016] Flight airspeed record, [Online] https://en.wikipedia.org/wiki/Flight_airspeed_record

PART THREE
What's next?

Future learning technologies 13

We always overestimate the change that will occur in the next two years and underestimate the change that will occur in the next ten.
BILL GATES, *THE ROAD AHEAD*, 1996

We began this book with a 1999 prediction about the future from John Chambers (see epigraph on page 7). I believe Chambers was right about the likely eventual massive impact of learning technologies. He was just wrong about the timing. As Microsoft co-founder Bill Gates pointed out a few years earlier, it is quite usual to be overenthusiastic about change in the short-term, and fail to see how broad it will be in the longer run.

One reason for this is that our understanding of what is possible is conditioned by our experience. That limits us. It makes us innovate in the shape of the past, which is why both the first cars and the first railway carriages were shaped like horse-drawn coaches.

Occasionally, someone is imaginative enough to alter the future by either creating something truly new or – more usually – combining existing technologies in a new way. These people are seldom the first movers, the original inventors. More usually they are in the next wave, who see a technology's potential. James Watt, for all his originality, did not invent the steam engine, but modified it brilliantly and so precipitated the Industrial Revolution. Apple did not invent the smartphone from scratch. As Mariana Mazzucato points out, it combined existing materials and processes in new ways with the addition of an exceptional user experience (Mazzucato, 2013).

If we were to think about the learning technology of the future by extrapolating from the past, through the present, we would hugely underestimate what the future holds. We would be left with the equivalent of the pitiful, wheezing, pre-Watt steam engines of Thomas Newcomen, or the clunky, handheld digital assistants before

Apple reimagined them. We would be stuck with further refinements of a model that has its roots in the schoolroom assumption, which sees learning technology as a way to parcel up, store and distribute information.

There is, however, little chance of such stasis. On the contrary, there is good reason to believe that the future will be different from today in ways that are almost impossible to predict – for evidence, just look back a few years. In the past decade or so we have seen the creation of: Facebook (2004), YouTube (2005), the iPhone, Twitter (both 2006), tablets (2010), Android (2010) and WhatsApp (2010) – the hardware and software that have transformed information sharing, learning and work. These innovations were built on the foundations of the previous decade, including broadband internet access, reliable Wi-Fi and powerful search algorithms.

Looking back over predictions of the future made around 2000, I have been unable to find anything that predicted social media, powerful, portable devices and in particular today's culture of sharing (and possibly over-sharing) information, experience and opinion. By extension, it would be folly today, in 2017, to attempt to predict the technologies that will change learning in the coming decades. Google co-founder Sergey Brin is wise enough to recognize this. If anyone should know about the future of artificial intelligence (AI), it is Brin, whose company has been at the forefront of developing AI, the technology most likely to completely alter how we live, work and learn. And yet, when asked to comment about the future of AI he replied that it was 'impossible to forecast accurately' (Naughton, 2017).

What we can do, however, is suggest trends, and point to evidence of these trends at work today. How exactly these trends finally make themselves manifest, and the precise technologies that emerge as a result, are less important than the overall direction of travel for learning and technology, which is towards a world abundant in content, with sophisticated curation and where algorithms and artificial intelligence create an invisible infrastructure to our lives in a way almost unimaginable today.

These three trends provoke a question, which we address in the final chapter of this book: Is the learning and development profession ready for a future of technology and learning quite unlike what has come before? Before we tackle that important challenge, though, we examine how these three trends are making themselves apparent today.

Evidence of the future today

The three technology trends that I believe will most affect workplace learning in the future are: the increased abundance of free or low-cost content, progressively more sophisticated means of curation, and a growing role for algorithms and artificial intelligence. Evidence of each can be seen in L&D today.

Abundant content

In Chapter 6 we explored the different types of content available to L&D professionals, and examined how we have moved rapidly from a position where the L&D department was responsible for creating the vast majority of learning content within organizations to where we are now: in a world superabundant in free and near-free information. The amount of content out there is only going to increase, something that the L&D profession can exploit, but often seems reluctant to.

There is some good reason for this reluctance. Not all internet content is – to put it mildly – useful for adults wishing to learn. Some content, however, is not only suitable, but is designed with that aim in mind. This includes Massive Open Online Courses (MOOCs). While these are not the only form of free or nearly free adult learning content available on the web, they are a good example of some current trends, and also of the reaction of L&D.

MOOCs exploded into public consciousness in 2012, as the result of what appeared to be a magical ability to attract money. In April, Coursera picked up US $16 million in funding; in May, MIT and Harvard jointly put US $60 million behind edX; in October, Udacity announced US $15 million in funding; in December, 12 major British universities combined to form FutureLearn.

The sudden, overnight successes of MOOCs in 2012 was, in reality, not sudden at all. Nor did everyone agree that they were particularly successful.

MOOCs had been with us since at least 2008, when Canadians George Siemens and Stephen Downes ran an online class in learning theory for the University of Manitoba, which more than 2,000 people showed up for. The term MOOC was coined to describe this new style of teaching by colleagues Dave Cormier and Bryan Alexander (Learn Canvas, 2013).

However, not all MOOCs are the same. Downes and Siemens' MOOCs involve people working together along the lines of their Connectivist approach to learning (Siemens, 2004), and are known as cMOOCs. Most of the well-funded courses run by universities and private institutions use an instructional model instead, and are known as xMOOCs.

As well as being far from an overnight success, they were not successful by some measures, because the schoolroom assumption is that the class enters on time, attends for the entire hour and leaves on the school bell. That is a completion rate of 100 per cent, even though attendance says nothing about learning. During their contentious early days, completion rates for MOOCs were frequently cited as being in the single percentage digits (Parr, 2013).

This has not stopped MOOCs gathering seemingly unstoppable momentum. If MOOCs were born in 2008 and hit the press in 2012, then 2015 was the year their use exploded. More people registered for MOOCs in 2015 than in the previous three years combined, with the number of people who had signed up for at least one course exceeding 35 million, up from 16–18 million the previous year. Importantly, this was the first year that the market grew faster than Coursera, the largest supplier, which increased its user base by 7 million to 17 million students in total (Shah, 2015). Provision has leapt, too. FutureLearn's original cohort of 12 universities has swollen to 64 worldwide, along with a further 47 partners.

And the MOOC model is evolving. Some providers are already moving away from the schoolroom model, and involving participants in a great deal of interaction. (FutureLearn stresses its courses work through storytelling, discussion, community support and social learning (FutureLearn, 2017).) Not all MOOCs are offered by universities now – some large corporations offer their own to both employees and non-employees in the 'extended enterprise' of supply chain and/or distribution and sales. Increasingly there is a range of approaches to costs, too. For some MOOCs a certificate of completion is an additional extra, available for a fee. For others an obligatory paid-for certificate has become a way of both reducing numbers and raising revenue. And amid all this change, the number of MOOCs on offer continues to increase: from near to zero in January 2012 to 4,000 in January 2016 (Shah, 2015).

Yet in the face of this growth and diversity of free or near-free material, the reaction of L&D has been largely a lack of interest. Every year, I run a worldwide poll of L&D professionals, asking what they think will be 'hot' in the following year. Respondents choose up to three options from a list. In 2014, MOOCs ranked fourth of 12 options. Each subsequent year this ranking has fallen, and by the 2017 Global L&D Sentiment Survey, 885 people from 60 countries placed MOOCs unequivocally last of 16 choices (Taylor, 2017). Largely, it seems, L&D is ignoring MOOCs, and this is a dangerous precedent. If L&D still sees the professional role as focused on the production of learning content, it will lose an opportunity to make the most of the growing amount of free material out there. It will also lose influence in the workplace, because people in the workplace will turn to MOOCs, or YouTube, or to other low-cost providers anyhow without approaching the L&D department at all. At that point, L&D will have become marginalized, confined to what I have elsewhere called the 'Training Ghetto', where interesting learning initiatives that will impact the business are carried out somewhere else in the enterprise, with the L&D department confined to a narrow role of induction, compliance and remedial training (Taylor, 2013).

Personalization, playlists and pathways

While I have focused on MOOCs, they are just one example of a trend towards an ever-increasing amount of good quality content being widely available at low cost or no cost. This abundance has led in turn to another trend: enabling better control and use of that content.

A 'playlist' was originally a collection of songs put together for an occasion like a party. Literally it was the list of the order in which to play the vinyl records. The idea has been extended and playlists of everything are everywhere. On YouTube you can find playlists of 1980s glam rock, of poetry for classrooms, of DIY videos and more. It was only a matter of time before the playlist reached workplace learning.

The obvious way to use a playlist is to assemble short pieces of content together to make a course, or something like one. It is already possible do this with providers like Lynda. Online learning company Lynda was bought by LinkedIn for US $1.5 billion in April 2015 (Kosoff, 2015), and provides a library of some 4,000 courses and a far larger number of video tutorials. (A year later, LinkedIn was in turn bought by Microsoft for US $26 billion (BBC, 2016).)

This is an impressive range of materials, but there is a problem with having too much choice. Not only can it be difficult to find what you want, it can actually be demotivating. Iyengar and Lepper's famous 2000 study of choosing – whether for jam, essay subjects or chocolates – showed that participants found selection easier, and were happier with their selections, when the choice was limited. In the essay study, a smaller range of options also led to them writing better essays (Iyengar and Lepper, 2000).

Playlists are the obvious response to the wide range of materials found in any collection of learning materials. Rather than simply giving people the keys to the library, give them the keys along with a reading list tailored to their needs. Lynda's playlist function enables combinations of materials which fit a particular need. These could be to support a particular role or a particular course, or a way of supporting a person in a particular location.

One large Irish company had its team of 35 trainers compile playlists both for personal development and to help employees work towards professional certifications. Looking at the usage data, they were able to modify the playlists based on what worked best for each job role, each team, and even according to what seemed to be most successful on each day of the week. Here, the trainers were not fulfilling their normal role of creating and delivering courses. They were instead using their valuable expertise to curate existing materials created by someone else.

It is not only internal L&D departments that are taking this curation role. Founded in 2012, US-based Degreed is one of a number of companies making it their business. Degreed acts as a super curator, pulling in courses from the likes of Lynda and elsewhere, as well as selected articles, papers and book extracts to make learning playlists from almost anything on the web, and track progression across them.

Picking a way across that range of materials can be a daunting task, which is where the playlists come it. Degreed has sets of playlists for individuals by role, by aim and by job title. It can also track reading as well as formal online and face-to-face courses, and firmly pitches itself against traditional learning systems.

Personalized playlists like this are a natural extension of the idea of curated content sets that we saw in Chapter 6, but taken to a new level of sophistication. That sophistication, however, is resource intensive to achieve. To work well at scale, it is not something that can be done practicably by hand.

Algorithms and artificial intelligence

How does Amazon know which book to suggest you read next? How does Netflix have an uncanny sense of your viewing tastes? How can Google suggest what you are going to type in that search box before you even finish? They all use algorithms, based on our usage patterns and those of millions of other users. The amount of personalization in the services we use every day is extraordinary, and yet we barely remark on it.

Given the proven success of algorithms in our daily life, many software providers are extending the same principle to learning in the workforce. London-based Filtered was founded in 2009, has a staff of about 30 and a US patent pending on its algorithm for identifying the course content that people don't know, yet really need. This start-up uses the same principles as Amazon and Google to suggest what will work best for individual users of the system.

Filtered has built the various techniques behind its successful approach from scratch, and has been relentless about testing and measuring the effectiveness of this approach. They point out that not only do adaptive courses take less time to complete (by an estimated 20–50 per cent), they are also more effective. In a controlled study across 3,000 users, those adopting the adaptive approach learned 26 per cent more than those using a one-size-fits-all course (Filtered, 2016).

The prospect of learning more, in less time, is something of a holy grail for anyone buying a learning technology, and is a distance away from the traditional approach of simply parcelling up and distributing information and calling it training. Once exposed to the effectiveness of an algorithm-driven approach, individual learners and their employers are unlikely to want to return to one-size-fits-all training.

Rather as Google rapidly overtook other search engines such as Alta Vista in the early 2000s to establish a dominant position, we can expect a battle of the algorithms in learning technology. And this will not just be about the careful, personalized delivery of learning content for individuals. A deep application of artificial intelligence will do much more than this.

Imagine a machine that could learn about your patterns of behaviour from following your diary, your online activity and scanning your mail. Imagine if you also shared with it your personal and professional goals. Such a machine would certainly be able to provide content tailored for your preferred times and ways of learning. If you had said you needed to know more about business finance to develop yourself at work, then it could find a way to assess what you already knew, and only provide material to build on that. It would deliver that material at a time and in a way that suited you. Perhaps on your morning commute you would prefer a podcast and at the weekends some reading.

But suppose it went further, and aligned your learning programme with your areas of unconscious incompetence – where you need to know, but don't know that you need to know. And perhaps it could also add in material as a result of what it knows about developments in your company, and in your area of professional work. This machine would aim to help you prepare for a future you could not anticipate by factoring in trends you were unable to see. In the long term, that would provide you with a compelling advantage over others in the same field.

Suppose it did not stop at providing access to content personalized for your needs, but also included performance support, and suggested you connect with particular experts who could help you develop through *ad hoc* conversation. This artificial intelligence machine would not be a Learning Management System that we turned to reluctantly when we needed to do our annual compliance training, it would be an invisible, seamless, part of our working lives, the antithesis of what poor Sally was struggling with in Starbucks.

In a world where artificial intelligence can beat expert humans not just at chess but also at poker (Naughton, 2017), detect a lie in an e-mail (Billington, 2016) and against the odds predict the outcome of the US presidential election (Engel, 2016), it is not merely credible that such a machine could be built, I would say it is inevitable. It is unlikely to be a single 'machine', but rather a series of services, offered by different providers. It will arrive piecemeal, rather than all at once, but arrive it will, and sooner than we think, for one compelling reason: it is good business. As human capital and intangible assets increasingly become the main differentiators for organizations, and as the capability of artificial intelligence rises and its costs fall, it is simply a matter of time before we see AI transforming how we learn. The question is not when it will happen, but rather who has the money and expertise to make it happen?

The future is different, large and well-funded

Traditionally, the learning technologies market has been highly fragmented and not particularly large. It has a few big players and plenty of smaller ones. Nobody knows how many LMS providers there are, but estimates put the number at over 500. There are tens of thousands of bespoke content providers worldwide. Some niche companies among these may be able to provide parts of the artificial intelligence learning solution of the future, but evidence suggests that the future of learning technologies may belong in the hands of the world's software giants.

In December 2015, Facebook founder Mark Zuckerberg announced that he and his wife planned to give away 99 per cent of their Facebook shares – currently valued at about US $45 billion – to a variety of causes, including software 'that understands how you learn best and where you need to focus' (Herold, 2016). He has already begun donations to trusts focused on schools, even though his 2010 donation of US $100 million to help schools in Newark is widely regarded as a failure (Russakoff, 2015). Whatever else happens, this level of funding and support will at the very least impact where other people decide to invest.

The key learning technology that Zuckerberg's company has backed is Oculus Rift, the virtual reality (VR) technology that Facebook bought in 2014 for US $2 billion (an eye-watering sum considering that the small company wasn't actually generating any sales at that stage). His explanation for the purchase underlines his commitment to learning and his long-term vision that enabled him to see beyond Oculus Rift's then focus on gaming. On Facebook, he wrote: 'Imagine… enjoying a court side seat at a game, studying in a classroom of students and teachers all over the world or consulting with a doctor face-to-face – just by putting on goggles in your home' (Zuckerberg, 2014). US $2 billion for a technology that is significantly focused on education and learning. That's a game changer.

However, it is also interesting to see how limited Zuckerberg's explanation was of the possible uses of VR technology for learning: 'Studying in a classroom of students and teachers'. This is, literally, the schoolroom assumption. Scottish learning technologist and blogger Donald Clark sees things differently. Writing after the acquisition, he pointed out 10 ways in which VR was already being used for learning, including putting yourself in someone else's shoes for diversity training, construction training and understanding physics better by trying a space-walk (Clark, 2014).

VR is just an example of one area of the substantial investment a software giant is willing to make to affect learning at work. What really matters is the influence of significant companies in this field, something that didn't happen at the beginning of the e-learning revolution. Facebook has Oculus Rift. Microsoft/LinkedIn has Lynda. Google has Google classroom (an administrative tool for teachers). More importantly, all of these companies also have an impressive understanding of the power of algorithms and artificial intelligence, a long history of using them and the resources to make them work.

If the idea of my invisible 'learning machine' sounds incredible, consider how utterly incredible and distant a self-driving car would have seemed in 2005. And yet now, in 2017, we have self-driving cars and lorries on trial on the road, close to mainstream production. And the main company behind that innovation – Google – is not in the automotive or transport businesses. But neither is it in the software business. Its mission statement makes that clear: 'Google's mission is to organize the world's information and make it universally accessible and useful' (Google, 2017). Put like that, it seems that Google is squarely in the learning business. It and other software giants are set to impact the future of learning technologies substantially, by direct investment and through acquisition. While their influence will be substantial and beneficial to enterprises and employees, it is also likely to be fundamentally disruptive to the L&D industry and profession.

A note of caution

It is impossible to consider any new technology without a combination of wonder and excitement at what it may make possible. However, it is also crucial to sound a note of caution.

We've been here before. In 1999 John Chambers suggested a grand vision for technology-supported learning. That vision failed to be realized. Instead we found click-next courses and frustration.

In his excellent *Geek Heresy*, Kentaro Toyama describes his journey from technophile to techno-realist, detailing a long series of recent instances in which technologies have failed to achieve their predicted impact, until the reader is compelled to ask why on earth we continue to make the same mistake of expecting technology to solve anything. He then points out our long history of such failings in the field of education, citing emeritus Stanford professor Larry Cuban's chronicle of failures past. These begin with Edison's belief (expressed in 1913) that 'The motion picture is destined to revolutionize our educational system'. In 1932, Benjamin Darrow claimed that radio would be 'a vibrant and challenging textbook of the air' and in the 1960s President Kennedy authorized US $32 million for classroom television programmes (Toyama, 2015).

It seems all we can learn from this is that humanity is destined never to learn from its own mistakes, however frequently repeated.

Although he describes himself as a 'recovering technoholic', Toyama does not claim that technology is evil or pointless. On the contrary, he gives many cases in which it has a positive effect. His point is that this is not an automatic result of implementing technology. Whether the impact is positive or negative depends on what was there beforehand. As he puts it: technology's primary effect is to amplify human forces. 'What people get out of technology depends on what they can do and want to do even without technology.'

This chapter began with a quote from Bill Gates. It will end with one, too, made 20 years before Toyama's book and which underscores his point. Gates, the co-founder of Microsoft, has lived through an amazing period of technical change and been responsible for a good part of it. In the course of his illustrious career he has accumulated a substantial fortune that he is now using to alleviate some of the worst conditions facing humanity – such as malaria – via the Bill and Melinda Gates Foundation.

In short, this man knows technology and knows that the world is far from perfect, but does not believe the former to be a panacea for the latter. Technology, he appreciates, is a selective power, to be used wisely, in the right circumstances.

In *The Road Ahead* – published years before John Chambers made his celebrated COMDEX speech – Gates wrote: 'The first rule of any technology used in a business is that automation applied to an efficient operation will magnify the efficiency. The second is that automation applied to an inefficient operation will magnify the inefficiency' (Gates *et al*, 1996).

Any learning and development professional who thinks things have changed dramatically since COMDEX 1999 is right. They should know, however, that this is only the beginning of a long, turbulent period of dramatic, technology-fuelled change with no end in sight. The plans of software giants such as Google and Facebook are evidence of that.

We must consider this unfolding technology landscape with Gates and Toyama in mind. We have to ask ourselves: How good are our current approaches to learning? Do we run the risk of making inadequate practice worse by applying technology? And that leads to deeper questioning: What shape will the future L&D profession take, and is everyone capable of adapting to it?

Key takeaways

1 One current trend that will have an impact in the future of learning technologies is the increasing amount of good quality content available at low or no cost.

2 Massive, Open, Online Courses (MOOCs) are one example of the increased amount of such content that will challenge the need of L&D to produce its own.

3 Amid this super abundance of free material, it will be time-consuming to find the most useful content. This issue will be reduced by the increased use of playlists and other methods of curation, sometimes associated with learning platforms.

4 Increasingly, playlists will be created not by people but by algorithms. It is likely that they will be created not *en masse*, but personalized for individuals.

5 The greatest single future trend in learning technology is likely to be the use of artificial intelligence across a range of different technologies and services.

6 Artificial intelligence in this field will be hugely influenced by global software giants such as Facebook, Google and Microsoft/LinkedIn.

References

BBC (2016) [accessed: 29 January 2017] Microsoft to buy LinkedIn for $26bn, [Online] http://www.bbc.co.uk/news/business-36519766

Billington, J (2016) [accessed: 29 January 2017] Researchers develop algorithm that can detect when you're lying in an email, *International Business Times*, 29 June, [Online] http://www.ibtimes.co.uk/how-spot-lie-email-algorithm-developed-by-researchers-detects-digital-deception-1568137

Clark, D (2014) [accessed 20 December 2016] 10 mind-blowing Oculus Rift experiments in education, [Online] http://donaldclarkplanb.blogspot.co.uk/2014/12/10-mind-blowing-oculus-rift-experiments.html

Engel, P (2016) [accessed: 29 January 2017] An artificial intelligence system that correctly predicted the last 3 elections says Trump will win,

Business Insider, 29 October, [Online] http://uk.businessinsider.com/artificial-intelligence-trump-win-2016-10

Filtered (2016) [accessed 20 December 2016] Approach, [Online] http://learn.filtered.com/approach

FutureLearn (2017) [accessed: 29 January 2017] Why it works, [Online] https://www.futurelearn.com/using-futurelearn/why-it-works

Gates, B, Myhrvold, N and Rinearson, P (1996) *The Road Ahead*, Penguin Books, London

Google, (2017) [accessed: 29 January 2017] Company overview, [Online] https://www.google.com/about/company/

Herold, B (2016) [accessed 20 December 2016] Facebook's Zuckerberg to Bet Big on Personalized Learning, *Education Week*, 7 March, [Online] http://www.edweek.org/ew/articles/2016/03/07/facebooks-zuckerberg-to-bet-big-on-personalized.html

Iyengar, S S and Lepper, M R (2000) When Choice is Demotivating: Can one desire too much of a good thing?, *Journal of Personality and Social Psychology*, 79 (6), pp 995–1006, doi: 10.1037//0022-3514.79.6.995

Kosoff, M (2015) [accessed 20 December 2016] LinkedIn just bought online learning company Lynda for $1.5 billion, *Business Insider*, [Online] http://uk.businessinsider.com/linkedin-buys-lyndacom-for-15-billion-2015-4?r=US&IR=T

Learn Canvas (2013) [accessed 20 December 2016] The Original MOOCs, [Online] https://learn.canvas.net/courses/4/pages/the-original-moocs

Mazzucato, M (2013) *The Entrepreneurial State: Debunking public vs. private sector myths*, Anthem Press, London

Naughton, J (2017) [accessed: 29 January 2017] No one can read what's on the cards for artificial intelligence, *The Guardian*, 29 January, [Online] https://www.theguardian.com/commentisfree/2017/jan/29/no-one-can-read-cards-artificial-intelligence-poker-libratus-sergey-brin

Parr, C (2013) [accessed 20 December 2016] Mooc completion rates 'below 7%', *Times Higher Education*, [Online] https://www.timeshighereducation.com/news/mooc-completion-rates-below-7/2003710.article

Russakoff, D (2015) [accessed 20 December 2016] $100 Million, Mark Zuckerberg, and a Controversial Education Experiment, *Education Week*, 9 September, [Online] http://www.edweek.org/ew/articles/2015/09/09/100-million-mark-zuckerberg-and-an-education-experiment.html

Shah, D (2015) [accessed 20 December 2016] By The Numbers: MOOCS in 2015, *Class Central*, [Online] https://www.class-central.com/report/moocs-2015-stats/

Siemens, G (2004) [accessed 20 December 2016] Connectivism: A learning theory for the digital age, *elearnspace*, [Online] http://www.elearnspace.org/Articles/connectivism.htm

Taylor, D (2013) [accessed: 29 January 2017] Are you in the Training Ghetto?, 15 April, [Online] http://donaldhtaylor.co.uk/are-you-in-the-training-ghetto/

Taylor, D (2017) [accessed: 29 January 2017] The L&D Global Sentiment Survey 2017, [Online] www.donaldhtaylor.co.uk/gss

Toyama, K (2015) *Geek Heresy: Rescuing social change from the cult of technology*, PublicAffairs, USA

Zuckerberg, M (2014) [accessed 20 December 2016] I'm excited to announce that we've agreed to acquire Oculus VR, the leader in virtual reality technology, *Facebook*, [Online] https://www.facebook.com/zuck/posts/10101319050523971

The future roles of L&D

14

We decided to stop being a course factory. JEFF KORTENBOSCH, 2016

Anybody can help somebody else get better at something. ANCA IORDACHE, 2016

Our story began in 1999, when e-learning was in its infancy. We end by considering how the L&D profession, and its relationship with learning technologies, will evolve in the future.

Technology and software today are so far removed from 1999, and changing so fast, and the techniques people use to learn at work have shifted so much, that in the second decade of this century the L&D community was driven into a fit of soul searching. Where, they wondered, was the profession heading?

Life without L&D?

In April 2016, Jane Hart (whom we met in the section on tools in Chapter 5) tackled this question head on. In a provocative Tweet that was retweeted 32 times, she posed the question: 'What would happen if there were no L&D department?' The consensus among the replies was that if L&D departments suddenly disappeared, the responsibility for learning would coalesce around individuals and teams, empowered as they now were to access content and learning tools online. However, Clark Quinn, a colleague of Jane's at the Internet Time Alliance (an international collective of L&D thinker/practitioners), added a rider, saying that people would eventually 'want to have some overarching principles to make into practices, and a new, sensible L&D would evolve' (Hart, 2016). It seemed there was consensus that learning and development at work were necessary and desirable, even if the L&D profession was dispensable.

Clark is the author of one of the many articles and books on L&D's role, which have been spawned by this period of change and debate. The theme of his *Revolutionize Learning and Development* is – as the title suggests – that the time has come to overturn much of what L&D has been doing. In the opening chapter, he paints a bleak picture, saying L&D has been 'a willing participant in complacency. As a consequence, L&D is on a steady path to extinction.' Despite this apocalyptic language, the rest of the book is immensely practical in suggesting ways that L&D can turn its game around and flourish. After all, as Clark notes in the same paragraph, L&D has the potential to be 'perhaps the most essential component of a business' (Quinn, 2014).

While I would agree with the potential of L&D, I do not believe things are quite as bleak as Clark's striking rhetoric suggests. Yes, L&D needs to adapt, but it will never become extinct. The choice is subtler and in some ways starker. It is the choice between evolving or being ignominiously sidelined. In many organizations today, this has already happened. L&D departments are increasingly tasked with doing more with no increase in resources, leaving them no time to explore the wider possibilities of their role. They find themselves reacting to the organization's demand for courses, on what seems to be an endless treadmill of content production. In turn this limits the time they have to explore other ways of adding to the business, and the department becomes focused only on onboarding and compliance training and on responding to demands for ad-hoc courses. This is not extinction, but it is certainly very far from Clark's vision of L&D fulfilling its potential as the most essential part of a business.

While this grim state of affairs is the reality for too many in L&D today, there is good news. Many L&D practitioners are doing good work, adding value to the business in practical ways and developing themselves at the same time. What are they doing that is different, and what can this tell us about the likely future state of the L&D profession?

We previously encountered Towards Maturity in Chapter 5. Their 2016–17 Learning Benchmark report is a 95-page document that looks at the successful implementation of digital learning in the workplace. Based on responses from 600 participants, the survey covers a lot of ground, including separating out the top 10 per cent of performers into what is called the 'Top Deck' of respondents. By definition, this Top Deck of performers will generally score higher on most measures in the survey than the rest of respondents. What is interesting is the size of the gap between them.

Of Top Deck L&D departments, 92 per cent say that in their organization 'Learning supports the skills the business needs', versus 62 per cent among the rest of survey respondents. The 30 per cent gap between these two may be no more than what we might expect. If the Top Deck is by definition the top tenth of respondents, the rest will be some way behind. Elsewhere, however, the gap is much larger and points towards what the successful L&D departments of tomorrow will be doing.

For example, 97 per cent of the Top Deck group say that their business leaders recognize the alignment of learning to business goals, against just 37 per cent of the rest. Of the Top Deck, 74 per cent proactively try to understand how staff learn, just 25 per cent of the rest do this, and 82 per cent of the Top Deck regularly communicate success to line managers – only 33 per cent of the rest do. Those three results are all about communication, with leaders, staff and managers. It seems that real, two-way communication, with active listening on both sides, is a strong differentiator between the top performing L&D departments and the others.

Looking at the bigger picture, the report divides the results of the comprehensive survey into five sections – 'improving efficiency', 'fine-tuning processes', 'boosting performance', 'cultivating agility' and 'influencing culture'. In the first three categories, the numbers of respondents successfully achieving the aim of the category decrease evenly by quartile. This even distribution suggests that the difference between each quartile is one of degree. The worst performing quartile is probably doing some of the same things as the top quartile, but not perhaps quite as well.

With the last two categories of responses, however – 'cultivating agility' and 'influencing culture' – the picture is different. In these, the top quartile of respondents is far ahead of the rest. The distribution of results forms a curve with a sharp uptick for the top quartile. For 'cultivating agility', the gap between first and second quartile is 20 per cent. For 'influencing culture' the gap is 17 per cent, with the remaining quartiles much closer together. To me this suggests that the best performing L&D departments have a qualitatively different approach to these areas. Whatever they are doing, it is different from the other departments and far more effective.

New L&D, new roles

Thinkers and practitioners in L&D have latched onto this idea that high-performing L&D departments are not doing things in traditional ways. Many use this as a leaping-off point for suggesting a new approach for L&D.

Dani Johnson, Research Manager, Learning and Development at Bersin and Deloitte, points to the amount of time L&D spends on content: 'Currently, L&D departments dedicate 40 percent of their resources to live delivery, and content design and development.' Dani makes a strong claim that L&D needs to develop a new mind set: 'L&D organizations are focusing more on becoming enablers of organizational learning, not just content providers...' One key focus for Dani is for L&D to move their organizations from seeing learning as a series of events towards her concept of Continuous Learning, which we encountered in Chapter 3 (Johnson, 2015).

Meanwhile, Charles Jennings in his substantial book on the 70:20:10 model (also seen in Chapter 3) suggests five new roles for L&D: the 'performance detective', 'performance architect', 'performance master builder', 'performance game changer' and 'performance tracker' (Arets, Jennings and Heijnen, 2015). Charles makes it clear, however, that these roles may not be intended solely for L&D professionals, but also for managers and other staff members. This idea that responsibility for L&D is likely to be shared with others outside a department suggests a new role for the specialist: 'It makes sense to work in teams at improving performance, with different people having different roles, managed by 70:20:10 experts who monitor the performance and results of the project.' It is quite possible that in the future, the L&D profession may be smaller, but more highly specialized, working closely with those in the business.

Jane Hart echoes this idea of a move away from a focus on content production and towards closer ties to the business: 'As we have seen, Modern Workplace Learning involves a new range of activities – it's no longer just about designing, delivering and/or managing courses anymore – but as much about working with managers, groups and individuals to help them learn in the ways that work best for them.' Like Charles Jennings, Jane makes the point that in the future, the L&D professional is likely to have three new areas of work: to modernize L&D-led learning, to support manager-led learning and to empower employee-led learning. Also like Charles, she suggests particular roles that will be relevant in the future, including those of curator, learning experience designer, facilitator, event organizer, collaboration advisor, community manager and learning advisor (Hart, 2017).

These three approaches share common themes also shared by others who have speculated on the future of the L&D department:

- L&D's main focus will move away from content production and delivery.
- It will be focused on performance as much as on learning.
- Learning will be embedded in work, rather than defined by training events.
- Responsibility for learning will be shared with managers and staff.
- As well as new skills, the new L&D department will need a new mindset.

In conjunction with this, the Towards Maturity survey tells us that true communication with all members of the organization will continue to be a trait of high-performing L&D departments. That particular skill, though, is in short supply in L&D. Research by the Learning and Performance Institute shows that communication continues to be one area where L&D professionals perform badly in a set of 27 skills defining modern L&D. The most widely held skills, perhaps unsurprisingly, are those of developing and delivering training materials (LPI, 2017).

Working with future learning technologies

In Chapter 5, we used Michael G Moore's three types of interaction to categorize learning technologies and in subsequent chapters focused on the first of them, the one emphasizing both the content that people work with and the technology that makes it accessible to them:

- Learner–Content
- Learner–Instructor/Expert
- Learner–Learner

The ways in which we share and source content using technology will continue to be important in the future, but the content will become more diverse, with fewer courses and more resources, and L&D's role will shift away from creating content and move towards managing it. In turn, we will see an increase in the amount of material sourced via both user-generated content (UGC) and curated content sets. And it is likely that these content sets will be curated by algorithms and artificial intelligence, as suggested in the previous chapter.

As we move away from a focus on producing content, so L&D's focus will shift to Moore's two other types of interaction: communication with experts and collaboration with peers. We will largely shift from being the guardians and gatekeepers of content to being the curators and facilitators of conversations, which in turn will create a large amount of valuable UGC.

To be effective in this new world of learning technologies, the L&D department is going to need the skills and mindset we have seen in the APPA approach of identifying a clear *aim*, retaining a strong *people* focus, ensuring a wide *perspective* and approaching any technology implementation with the right *attitude*.

The right skills

Drawing on what we have covered in the section above, and looking back over the content of Part Two of this book, there are many skills that tomorrow's L&D department will need to deal with learning technologies in the future. Of these, I believe the three essential skills to be:

- performance consulting – to uncover what the real issues are;
- active listening – to understand what people really mean;
- real communications – to engage in-depth with the business, over time.

These are all closely related, have nothing to do with technology and everything to do with people. There is a good reason for this. L&D has too often allowed itself to be beguiled and distracted by technology and paid too little attention to those whom the technology serves. Learning, ultimately, is always about people, whether technology is involved or not.

The right mindset

Unsurprisingly, much of this mindset for dealing with learning technology rests on what we have already touched on in the chapters on perspective and attitude. Its core attributes are:

- a curiosity and openness to new ideas – to constantly maintain a wide perspective;
- a high tolerance of ambiguity – because we live in a world of incomplete information;
- a willingness to be challenged – to gather useful feedback which improves practice;
- an openness to some level of risk – because playing safe is a recipe for failure;
- a willingness to let go of control – to stop L&D being a brake on learning.

While the other points on this list have all appeared in the chapters on attitude and perspective, the last point did not. It may not be necessary to implement any particular learning technology at the moment, but it will be increasingly necessary as part of L&D's role in the future, as Dani Johnson, Charles Jennings and Jane Hart have all pointed out. Remember how Jeremy Smith ceded maintenance of Herman Miller's EPSS to those people directly concerned with operations. In the future, increasingly, learning technologies are likely to be so embedded into work that the idea of a non-operational entity controlling them will be regarded as both impractical and bizarre. Learning using technology will simply be part of how we live and work.

The future is already here

A favourite quote for anyone contemplating the future is William Gibson's pithy 'The future is already here – it's just not evenly distributed.' He is right. Much of what I have been portraying as the skillsets and mindsets of the future are already in evidence in L&D today if you look hard enough. Indeed, one reason I have a positive view of the future of L&D is that I am lucky enough in my work to meet people who are already working as if the future were here. I would have used Gibson's quote at the start of this final chapter of this book, but for the fact that I met two such people just as I was wrapping up my manuscript prior to publication.

The quotes at the beginning of this chapter come from two L&D professionals with whom I shared a panel at the Online Educa Berlin conference in December 2016, and who express very neatly the way L&D is likely to operate differently in the future, underpinned by technology.

Jeff Kortenbosch is Senior e-Learning Specialist at AkzoNobel, a leading global paints, coatings and chemicals company, headquartered in the Netherlands, where he supports learning across all the organization's global business functions. Jeff told the story of moving his organization towards a way of learning that was more flexible and business-focused. His key point in reintroducing the concept of 70:20:10 into AkzoNobel was his realization that the L&D department needed to stop responding positively to every request for training and focus instead on performance. As Jeff put it, his team had to 'stop being a course factory'. This would not have been possible by simply refusing to deliver training. Instead, Jeff engaged the senior management in his organization about the new approach and won their enthusiastic support.

As part of Jeff's approach, he introduced Mosher and Gottfredson's concept of the five moments of learning need to set a new understanding of the limits of formal training. This provided the language for discussing when a course might be the answer to a performance issue, as well as pointing to all the times when it wasn't. This new emphasis on performance was underlined by running a proof of concept for an EPSS and selecting one. At the same time, Jeff began a process of auditing and developing the skills of his L&D team.

According to Jeff, the result of all this activity is that the first global 70:20:10 solutions are now being rolled out and that his internal clients at AkzoNobel are enthusiastic about using them as an alternative to training, something inconceivable a year earlier.

We have talked about the need for learning technologists to have a propensity for action, to want to make things happen. Jeff achieved this shift in the attitude of his organization in just one year, driven by an approach that expresses this propensity very well. He asks himself daily this question: 'What change can you make today that will impact tomorrow?'

Someone else who managed to shift an organization's view of learning is Anca Iordache at Citi, the global bank. A Romanian based at Citi's Swiss office, Anca was a lead player in a team that introduced a programme to change the way people thought about learning. The bank had found that courses alone were not helping people learn what they needed fast enough. The reason: L&D's role producing them was acting as a bottleneck on the flow of knowledge. As Anca puts it, 'We realized that all the knowledge and skills we need are widely distributed across the organization, and that anybody can help somebody else get better at something.' The answer was to enable people to share information and knowledge faster between themselves in the context of their work. A culture-campaign programme was born that Citi called #BeMore. Again, it used the idea of 70:20:10, but positioned in a way that would make sense throughout the bank without the need for further explanation. Citi expressed it as 'Experience, Exposure and Education'.

As we saw in Chapter 11, sharing information between employees by utilizing a social networking platform can be very effective, and indeed Citi's Jive-based Citi Collaborate platform reached about 12,000 employees within six months of its launch in mid-2015. However, simply introducing a platform by itself is never enough, and it was only one tool of the overall campaign to shift the learning culture of the organization. #BeMore also included the 30 Day Development Challenge, asking those on the platform to complete one 10-minute micro-action of self-development each day, for one month. This could be finding and talking to a new colleague, or reflecting on useful advice they may have received in the past. The kicker – they then had to share their thoughts about the actions they took and their impact on the platform. In the short space of time, 4,500 of them had.

By providing the platform and giving a clearly laid-out reason to use it, Citi precipitated a new way of thinking among employees and kick-started the habit of knowledge sharing, which in the great majority of cases continued after people had finished their 30-day challenge. Not only is the platform now in wide use for knowledge sharing, there has been a sharp rise in the number of completed Individual Development Plans. #BeMore has also produced, according to Anca, a lasting change in the way people feel about their own development, they are positive and more likely to take control themselves. One plus is that, like the staff at AkzoNobel, they are now less likely to seek out a course as their first answer to a performance problem.

Brian Murphy, Citi's head of L&D for EMEA puts it this way: 'L&D are not the fount of all knowledge and our traditional approaches no longer work. It was critical to shift to new learning principles, and pivot our role as learning professionals. In our team our priority was to shift to role of performance consultants. Our role in helping our people understand how to balance their own learning across the 3 E's – Experience, Exposure and Education – has been fundamental in supporting business change and agility in our organisation' (Overton, 2016).

Brian Murphy summarizes the long journey we have made, and the point we have reached, very well. The future will need a more self-assured and more widely capable learning and development profession, one that has above all the ability to work closely with the rest of the business. Perhaps in 1999 it was possible to consider learning technologies as something separate from the organization, a sort of platform for knowledge that could be installed and left to run like a piece of machinery. Whether that was true or not then, it is certainly not true now. As we have seen over the course of this book, how we work, how learning technologies are used, and the culture of an organization are all deeply intertwined. The common factor running through them all, the place where any workplace learning technology implementation starts and finishes, and the determining factor of its success, is always the same and will never change. Success in learning technologies depends on just one thing: people.

Key takeaways

1 There is evidence that top performing L&D departments do an outstanding job in communicating with leaders, managers and staff.

2 They also appear to be disproportionately more successful than their peers at cultivating agility and influencing culture in their organizations.

3 Among those thinking about the changing shape of L&D there is a broad consensus that traditional approaches will no longer be sufficient in the future.

4 In the future, successful L&D departments will no longer focus on the production and delivery of content.

5 Future L&D departments will have an explicit focus on performance.

6 They will change the perception of learning, and its workplace support, from an emphasis on events to the sense that learning is embedded in work.

7 They will share responsibility for learning and performance with managers and staff.

8 They will be exemplary at good communication at all levels of the organization.

9 Among the key skills of the future L&D department are an ability to carry out performance consulting and the related skill of active listening.

10 L&D will need to develop not only new skills to support these new ways of working, but also a new mindset.

11 This new mindset has many facets, but perhaps the most important part is a willingness to cede control of the learning process to the managers and employees it most directly affects.

12 Fortunately, there are L&D professionals currently demonstrating this mindset and these skills, and willing to share what they are doing.

References

Arets, J, Jennings, C and Heijnen, V (2015) *702010: Towards 100% performance*, Sutler Media, Maastrict

Hart, J (2016) [accessed 12 December 2016] What would happen if there were no L&D department? [Online] http://www.c4lpt.co.uk/blog/2016/04/07/what-would-happen-if-there-were-no-ld-department/

Hart, J (2017) *Learning in the Modern Workplace*, Centre for Learning and Performance Technologies, UK

Johnson, D (2015) *Reimagining L&D Capabilities to Drive Continuous Learning*, Bersin by Deloitte, Deloitte Consulting LLP

LPI (2017) *LPI Capability Map Report, 2017*, Learning and Performance Institute, Coventry

Overton, L (2016) [accessed 12 December 2016] Supporting a Shift in Learning Culture at Citi, [Online] http://www.towardsmaturity.org/article/2016/03/09/supporting-shift-learning-culture-citi/

Quinn, C N (2014) *Revolutionize Learning and Development: Performance and innovation strategy for the information age*, Pfeiffer, USA

Webinars, workshops, further case studies and other materials relating to the areas covered in this book can be found at **www.donaldhtaylor.co.uk**

INDEX

Note: 'chapter references' and 'key takeaways' are indexed as such; page numbers in *italics* indicate Figures or Tables.

CPSIA information can be obtained
at www.ICGtesting.com
Printed in the USA
BVHW04s1416150318
510681BV00005B/57/P

9 780749 476403